ARCO
Literary Critiques

D. H. Lawrence

Tony Slade, M.A.

New York

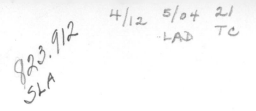

To My Grandfather, B. G. Baker

Published 1970 by ARCO PUBLISHING COMPANY, Inc.
219 Park Avenue South, New York, N.Y. 10003
Copyright © Tony Slade, 1969, 1970
All Rights Reserved
Library of Congress Catalog Number 78-101769
Printed in the United States of America

Arco Literary Critiques

Of recent years, the ordinary man who reads for pleasure has been gradually excluded from that great debate in which every intelligent reader of the classics takes part. There are two reasons for this: first, so much criticism floods from the world's presses that no one but a scholar living entirely among books can hope to read it all; and second, the critics and analysts, mostly academics, use a language that only their fellows in the same discipline can understand.

Consequently criticism, which should be as 'inevitable as breathing'—an activity for which we are all qualified—has become the private field of a few warring factions who shout their unintelligible battle cries to each other but make little communication to the common man.

Arco Literary Critiques aims at giving a straightforward account of literature and of writers—straightforward both in content and in language. Critical jargon is as far as possible avoided; any terms that must be used are explained simply; and the constant preoccupation of the authors of the Series is to be lucid.

It is our hope that each book will be easily understood, that it will adequately describe its subject without pretentiousness so that the intelligent reader who wants to know about Donne or Keats or Shakespeare will find enough in it to bring him up to date on critical estimates.

Even those who are well read, we believe, can benefit from a lucid exposition of what they may have taken for granted, and perhaps—dare it be said?—not fully understood.

K. H. G.

D. H. Lawrence

The aim of this book is to provide a balanced introduction to D. H. Lawrence, whose work is so powerful and many-sided that it is clearly impossible to do justice to it in one volume, whether large or small. I have therefore directed the reader's attention to the novels, through which Lawrence made his tremendous impact on 20th-century society. It is certainly no exaggeration to say that his is one of the great formative influences on our moral climate today, with his insistence on honesty, frankness and freedom of expression of the deepest instincts in man.

I regret that space has not allowed me to deal with his criticism (both social and literary) in a direct way, nor to make any mention of the travel books.

I have used the Heinemann Phoenix uniform edition for the novels and stories and for the quotations from *Fantasia of the Unconscious* and *Studies in Classic American Literature*, to which all chapter and page numbers refer, but I should have preferred to use the Penguin edition of the novels had these been uniformly available to me. The references to Lawrence's poems are to *The Complete Poems of D. H. Lawrence* in two volumes (edited by Vivian de Sola Pinto and Warren Roberts, Heinemann, 1964); references to Lawrence's essays are to *Phoenix* (edited by E. D. McDonald, Heinemann, reprinted edition 1961).

I should like to take this opportunity of thanking my colleagues and students at the University of Adelaide for their help in the writing of this book. Even more particularly I am grateful to my wife Jean and to Kenneth Grose, the General Editor of the series, for their sensible and often unconflicting advice at all stages of the manuscript.

T. S.

4

Contents

The Author

Tony Slade, M.A., is Senior Lecturer in English Literature at the University of Adelaide.

Acknowledgements

The author and publishers are indebted to Laurence Pollinger Limited and the Estate of the late Mrs. Frieda Lawrence for permission to quote from the poetry, letters, novels, essays, short stories and short novels of D. H. Lawrence, published in Great Britain by William Heinemann Limited. They are also indebted to The Viking Press Inc. for U.S.A. permission to quote extracts which are detailed below. From *The Complete Poems of D. H. Lawrence*, edited by Vivian de Sola Pinto and F. Warren Roberts, 'Nottingham's New University' (Volume I), copyright 1929 by Frieda Lawrence Ravagli; 'Piano' (Volume I), copyright 1920 by B. W. Huebsch Inc., renewed 1948 by Frieda Lawrence; 'Snake' (Volume I), copyright 1923, renewed 1951 by Frieda Lawrence; 'Innocent England' (Volume II), copyright © 1964 by Angelo Ravagli and C. Montague Weekley, Executors of the Estate of Frieda Lawrence Ravagli; 'In a Spanish Tram-car' (Volume II), copyright 1933 by Frieda Lawrence. From *The Collected Letters of D. H. Lawrence*, edited by Harry T. Moore, letter to J. D. Chambers, 14th November, 1928 and the letter to Edward Garnett, 5th June, 1914, copyright 1932 by the Estate of D. H. Lawrence. Copyright © renewed 1960 by Angelo Ravagli and C. Montague Weekley, Executors of the Estate of Frieda Lawrence Ravagli. From *The Rainbow* copyright 1915 by David Herbert Lawrence, renewed 1943 by Frieda Lawrence. From *Women in Love*, copyright 1920, 1922 by David Herbert Lawrence, renewed 1948, 1950 by Frieda Lawrence. From *Sons and Lovers*, copyright 1915 by Thomas Seltzer, Inc. From *Kangaroo*, copyright 1923 by Thomas Seltzer, Inc., renewed 1951 by Frieda Lawrence. From *Fantasia of the Unconscious*, copyright 1922 by Thomas Seltzer, Inc., renewed 1950 by Frieda Lawrence. From *Phoenix: The Posthumous Papers of D. H. Lawrence*, edited by Edward D. McDonald 'Study of Thomas Hardy' and 'Autobiographical Fragment', copyright 1936 by Frieda Lawrence, copyright © renewed 1964 by the Estate of the late Frieda Lawrence Ravagli. From *The Complete Short Stories of D. H. Lawrence* 'Daughters of the Vicar' (Volume I) and 'Odour of Chrysanthemums' (Volume II). From *Four Short Novels*, *The Captain's Doll*, copyright 1923 by Thomas Seltzer, Inc., renewed 1951 by Frieda Lawrence. From *The Portable D. H. Lawrence*, edited by Diana Trilling, *The Fox*, copyright 1923 by Thomas Seltzer, Inc., renewed 1951 by Frieda Lawrence. The extract from 'Apropos of Lady Chatterley's Lover' is reprinted by kind permission of Alfred A. Knopf, Inc. The extract from *The Good Soldier*, from *The Bodley Head Ford Madox Ford*, Volume I, edited by Graham Greene, is reprinted by kind permission of The Bodley Head and David Higham Associates, Ltd.

The portrait on the cover from the Lawrence Collection, Nottingham Public Libraries, is reproduced by kind permission of the City Librarian. The painting by Kai Gotzsche is reproduced by kind permission of the Humanities Research Center, The University of Texas at Austin. The photograph of Frieda Lawrence is reproduced by kind permission of Mr. Montague Weekley.

I

Life and Background

Although D. H. Lawrence has by now been widely accepted as one of the finest and most interesting of English novelists his real genius was consistently questioned and ridiculed during his lifetime, and indeed for some twenty years after his death, whilst critics and former acquaintances argued over his merits and faults, and censors in a number of free and democratic nations did their best to prevent some of his work ever being read at all. Few writers in modern English literature have stirred up so much uncritical admiration and vilification, and although this can partly be attributed to the personality of Lawrence himself, it is principally due to the subject which he chose for the basis of most of his novels, the last remaining taboo of our civilisation. The personal recriminations and recollections of the era between the two World Wars have now passed into history and would best be forgotten, were it not for the fact that the more ridiculous and extreme comments thrown at Lawrence affected his reputation amongst the reading public, and still influence it to some extent. Derogatory epithets such as 'a sex-soaked genius' (from a contemporary journalist shortly before his death) or, hardly more literate, 'sick, muddle-headed, sex-mad D. H. Lawrence' (from a modern poet, whose reputation is otherwise well worth preserving, and who is consequently best left anonymous) have affected the way in which Lawrence, arguably the finest English novelist of our century, has been regarded by many readers. His admirers too have not always been an asset to him, for the tendency of some of his more devoted apologists before the Second World War to see him as the religious and moral 'saviour' of our age is palpably far-fetched and certainly did him more harm than good.

Lawrence's writing, often for the wrong reasons, has reached many people who would be totally ignorant of other important modern literary figures, and the reaction of many people towards reading a novel such as *Lady Chatterley's Lover* has created in the public mind a confused folk-consciousness of the man and his work which even the thousand-odd critical and biographical works published on him since his death have done little to disperse. In one sense the controversy which has surrounded Lawrence arose out of a misunderstanding of what he was actually saying, and also out of a confusion between a dislike of his pronounced moral attitudes, especially towards sex, and a consequent inability to perceive the amazing literary genius with which these attitudes are portrayed in the novels and stories. Another cause of confusion and misunderstanding was Lawrence's educational and class background, which presented critics in the years between the wars (and occasionally since) with the problem of accounting for the emergence of a writer of genius who had none of their middle-class advantages of background and education. Consequently they took to patronising him, for as he himself wrote: 'In the early days they were always telling me I had got genius as if to console me for not having their own inestimable advantages.' Perhaps the most extreme example of this patronising tone occurred in a British Council pamphlet on D. H. Lawrence in which Kenneth Young wrote, incredibly, that Lawrence's

> 'dogmatic insistence that he alone held the truth about the universe surely reflects a deep-seated feeling that he had missed the fruits of the normal public school and university education, which gave his literary contemporaries a breadth of knowledge and assurance that he always lacked.'

(quoted from pp. 16–17 of the original 1952 edition of this pamphlet. The remark has been amended in later editions). The ridiculous assumptions implicit in this comment can be allowed to condemn themselves, but the quotation does give an example of the level at which some former commentators have discussed Lawrence's background. Lawrence was no doubt a puzzle to many of his more conventional contemporaries, but the English social revolution has ponderously developed slightly since his time, and today's readers and critics are a little less likely to wonder at the ability of the working-class product of an elementary school than were many of those then.

The class question is important in understanding Lawrence's work, both for itself and for its effect on Lawrence's relationship with his contemporaries. The middle- and upper-class friends he made later in his life were often upset and puzzled by what appeared to be his cantankerous and illogical rejection of their values and their qualified friendship. His former acquaintances in his home village of Eastwood were angered and suspicious of what seemed to them to be his rejection of their life in the portraits of Nottinghamshire and working-class life in the novels; it is still rumoured to be highly dangerous for the over-earnest pilgrim in Eastwood to disclose his intention too openly to some elements of the local populace, who still hold on resolutely to the belief that in his work Lawrence had insulted them or their parents or their background. Norman Shrapnel has an amusing, yet also in a way saddening, account of a visit to Eastwood in 1955 in which Lawrence is remembered:

> The first man I spoke to (in the Breach)—a young-old veteran of the pits properly dressed in flat cap and collarless shirt, 43 years a miner and twice badly injured—was swift off the mark.
> 'Bert Lawrence? Don't talk to me about him.' He gripped my elbow with a hard hand, and gave his judgment.
> 'I'd put him down as nowt. Given a tip-top education by his father—as fine a man as you'd meet in a day's march. That was on a butty's pay, pound to fifty shilling a week. Then he took all his knowledge away. Didn't give this country a penny back.'
> He brooded fiercely and then went on. 'Spoke to nobody. Never had a pal in his life. Only played ring-o-roses with young women.' At this improbable idyll of memory his spectacles shone in the afternoon sun like signal lamps across half a century.
> 'But his father, now there was a man. Full of life and friendliness.

Big roaring carnation in his coat. They still talk about him in Eastwood.' He pointed a hundred yards up the hill, as if to another world. 'He could dance, too, till his legs were broke to bits. He got buried.' This was announced with professional casualness; then he reverted to the shortcomings of the man whom the rest of the world, outside the Breach, regards as great. 'But Bert never acknowledged him properly, not as a father should be. It was the mother. Thought that much of herself. But she was nothing.'

The Manchester Guardian 18 March 1955

Since the plays of John Osborne and Arnold Wesker, and Richard Hoggart's *The Uses of Literacy*, however, most readers today can understand Lawrence's position sympathetically, and can understand that he stood for values of some importance in a world whose traditional values were fast changing.

EASTWOOD: 1885–1912

D. H. Lawrence was born on 11 September 1885 at Eastwood, a small mining village then some eight miles north-west of Nottingham, now inextricably caught up in Nottingham's vast suburban sprawl. Many of the main features of Lawrence's early life are dealt with in the partly-autobiographical novel *Sons and Lovers*, and these will be discussed further in another chapter, but it should be remembered that the novel does not claim to be an exact or entirely accurate autobiographical portrait. It is also worth remembering that in his lifetime Lawrence saw and felt keenly the changes made in the English landscape by the onrush of the later stages of the Industrial Revolution, and that Eastwood was at the time of his early life still relatively rural. As Lawrence himself explains in the essay 'Nottingham and the Mining Countryside':

> I was born ... in Eastwood, a mining village of some three thousand souls, about eight miles from Nottingham, and one mile from the small stream, the Erewash, which divides Nottinghamshire from Derbyshire. It is hilly country, looking west to Crich and towards Matlock, sixteen miles away, and east and north-east towards Mansfield and the Sherwood Forest district. To me it seemed, and still seems, an extremely beautiful countryside, just between the

red sandstone and the oak-trees of Nottingham, and the cold limestone, the ash-trees, the stone fences of Derbyshire. To me, as a child and a young man, it was still the old England of the forest and agricultural past; there were no motor-cars, the mines were, in a sense, an accident in the landscape, and Robin Hood and his merry men were not very far away. PHOENIX, p. 133

The change which Lawrence saw affecting this landscape is well brought out by comparing this passage with a later description in the posthumous 'Autobiographical Fragment':

Nothing depresses me more than to come home to the place where I was born, and where I lived my first twenty years, here, at New-thorpe, this coal-mining village on the Nottingham-Derby border. The place has grown but not very much, the pits are poor. Only it has changed. There is a tram-line from Nottingham through the one street, and buses to Nottingham and Derby. The shops are bigger, more plate-glassy: there are two picture-palaces, and one Palais de Danse.

But nothing can save the place from the poor, grimy, mean effect of the Midlands, the little grimy brick houses with slate roofs, the general effect of paltriness, smallness, meanness, fathomless ugliness, combined with a sort of chapel-going respectability. It is the same as when I was a boy, only more so.

Now, it is all tame. It was bad enough, thirty years ago, when it was still on the upward grade, economically. But then the old race of miners were not immensely respectable. They filled the pubs with smoke and bad language, and they went with dogs at their heels. There was a sense of latent wildness and unbrokenness, a weird sense of thrill and adventure in the pitch-dark Midland nights, and roaring footballing Saturday afternoons. The country in between the colliery regions had a lonely sort of fierceness and beauty, half-abandoned, and threaded with poaching colliers and whippet dogs. Only thirty years ago. PHOENIX, p. 817

Admittedly this is a common enough experience in 20th-century England; generations later, Arthur Seaton, the hero of Alan Sillitoe's novel *Saturday Night and Sunday Morning* (which is also centred on the Nottingham area) makes a similarly nostalgic complaint at the end of the book; but in Lawrence's case the

11

distress he feels at the changes taking place as a result of industrialisation has important consequences in his work.

Lawrence's father was a miner in the local colliery, and his marriage to Lydia Beardsall was not a successful one. She had been a school-teacher and came of a family which had been reasonably well-to-do, whilst the father's background was purely working-class. The class conflicts which are played out in much of Lawrence's work originate partly from the conflicts between the parents which continually shattered the domestic life of the family, with the mother insisting on the children being educated in a manner and to an extent which exceeded the father's wishes. In this respect the situation described in *Sons and Lovers* is an accurate one, but Lawrence came to feel in later life that during his childhood and in that novel itself he had been unsympathetic and unfair to his father. (The only virtue of the 1960 film version of the novel lay in the portrayal of the father by Trevor Howard, which allowed some scope for an understanding of the father's awkward family position.)

Lawrence was the second-to-youngest child of a family of five, and of all the children was the one with the most intense relationship with the mother. This relationship, which is central to *Sons and Lovers*, needs no further analysis here, but an interesting commentary on it and the novel itself is given in two highly illuminating studies of Lawrence's early life: E. T.'s *D. H. Lawrence, A Personal Record*, and Ada Lawrence's and G. Stuart Gelder's *Early Life of D. H. Lawrence*. 'E. T' is the pseudonym of Jessie Chambers, the Miriam of *Sons and Lovers*, and her recollections are by way of being a minor classic. Along with Lawrence's mother, Jessie Chambers was the dominating influence of his early life, and it was she who encouraged his writing and who helped to get his first work published. Lawrence often visited the Chambers family at the Haggs Farmhouse, a short distance in the countryside from Eastwood, and it was from Jessie and the rest of her family that he was to gain so much intellectually and generally, as he always acknowledged. In a letter to J. D. Chambers (Jessie's brother David) of 14 November 1928, Lawrence recalled his life with them:

Whatever I forget, I shall never forget the Haggs—I loved it so. I loved to come to you all, it really was a new life began in me there. The water-pippin by the door—those maiden blush roses that Flower would lean over and eat and trip floundering round.— And stewed figs for tea in winter, and in August green stewed apples. Do you still have them? Tell your mother I never forget, no matter where life carries us.—And does she still blush if somebody comes and finds her in a dirty white apron? Or doesn't she wear work-aprons any more? Oh, I'd love to be nineteen again, and coming up through the Warren and catching the first glimpse of the buildings. Then I'd sit on the sofa under the window, and we'd crowd round the little table to tea, in that tiny little kitchen I was so at home in. . . . If there is anything I can ever do for you, do tell me.—Because whatever else I am, I am somewhere still the same Bert who rushed with such joy to the Haggs.

H. T. Moore, LETTERS, vol. 2, p, 1100

In 1901 Lawrence left school and went to work for a surgical-appliance manufacturer in Nottingham, as Paul Morel does in *Sons and Lovers*, but Lawrence only remained in this employment for a few months. Later in the same year he became seriously ill with pneumonia, and after recovering slowly from this he became a pupil-teacher in Eastwood and then attended a pupil-teacher centre at Ilkeston from 1903–1905. Lawrence drew on his experiences at Ilkeston in the vivid descriptions of Ursula's teaching career in Chapter XIII of *The Rainbow*, where the stultifying atmosphere of elementary school conditions in the early years of this century are shown as dispiritingly demeaning to both staff and pupils. Like Ursula too, Lawrence left the pupil-teaching centre after receiving a grant to attend Nottingham University College, for whilst at Ilkeston he had sat for the King's Scholarship examination in 1904, and had come out first in the order of merit in the whole of England and Wales. The parallel between Lawrence's probable experiences at Nottingham University College from 1906–1908 and Ursula's as they are described in Chapter XV of *The Rainbow* is continued in her disillusionment there. She goes to college with vague yet idealistic notions of the value of knowledge and education to supply meaning to life:

Term began. She went into town each day by train. The cloistered quiet of the college began to close around her.

She was not at first disappointed. The big college built of stone, standing in the quiet street, with a rim of grass and lime trees all so peaceful: she felt it remote, a magic land. . . . Her soul flew back to the medieval times, when the monks of God held the learning of men and imparted it within the shadow of religion. In this spirit she entered college. p. 430

These ideals were too fragile to stand up to the reality of the situation for long. A feeling of the 'sterile degradation' of the institution came over her as she felt that it could not begin to supply her with a sense of purpose:

But during this year the glamour began to depart from college. The professors were not priests initiated into the deep mysteries of life and knowledge. After all, they were only middle-men handling wares they had become so accustomed to that they were oblivious of them. . . . The life went out of her studies, why, she did not know. But the whole thing seemed sham, spurious; spurious Gothic arches, spurious peace, spurious Latinity, spurious dignity of France, spurious naïveté of Chaucer. It was a second-hand dealer's shop, and one bought equipment for an examination. This was only a little side-show to the factories of the town. Gradually the perception stole into her. This was no religious retreat, no perception of pure learning. It was a little apprentice-shop where one was further equipped for making money. The college itself was a little, slovenly laboratory for the factory.

A harsh and ugly disillusion came over her again, the same darkness and bitter gloom from which she was never safe now, the realisation of the permanent substratum of ugliness under everything. pp. 434–5

The assumptions underlying Ursula's rejection of the college are certainly open to debate and qualification, but here we need only draw on the similarity between Ursula's position and Lawrence's own.

One subject which Lawrence had found useful and interesting at the University College was French, which was taught by Professor Ernest Weekley. Lawrence left Nottingham in 1908, and went to teach in Croydon, south of London, but he was again to come into contact with Weekley a few years later with important and far-reaching consequences for both men. Meanwhile, Lawrence's mother died in December 1910, and the first and most binding of his links with his home background was irrevocably shattered. *The White Peacock*, his first novel, published shortly after his mother's death in January 1911 was a mild success with the critics, and dealt almost exclusively with the Nottinghamshire rural countryside. The next novel, *The Trespasser*, was published the following year and drew on his experiences at Croydon, but the actual publication of this novel was completely overshadowed by the dramatic events taking place in his own life.

MARRIAGE AND THE WAR: 1912–1919

Lawrence gave up teaching in Croydon early in 1912, and had some idea of finding a teaching position at a German university. Accordingly he went to see his former Professor of French, Ernest Weekley, to obtain his advice. Weekley's wife Frieda, who was German by birth and the daughter of Baron Friedrich von Richthofen, was soon attracted to Lawrence and he to her. Quickly, and within a few weeks of meeting in Nottingham, Lawrence and Frieda left for Germany in May 1912. In reality this marked the end of Frieda's marriage to Weekley, and the beginning of her life-long relationship with the young author.

Lawrence's elopement with a married woman older than himself gave much scope to scandalmongers in later years, who professed to see it as the consequence of his supposedly 'perverted' and immoral sexual ideas destroying the sanctity of a happy marriage. In fact, only the strictest of puritans would today suggest Lawrence's relationship with Frieda to be in any way deplorable. Frieda had not been happy with Weekley, but she was to find meaning in her life with Lawrence. This is not to imply that the marriage of Lawrence and Frieda was perfect, for it was often far from being so, but, as Frieda wrote in later life, 'with Lawrence it was always worthwhile, even at the worst'. The significance of the relationship is evidenced by the importance of the theme of marriage in Lawrence's two greatest novels, *The Rainbow* and *Women in Love*.

Lawrence lived with Frieda from 1912, although the actual wedding ceremony did not take place until her divorce was finalised in 1914, and the relationship marks the major break in his life between the early Nottinghamshire world of his childhood and youth and his later career. Publication of *Sons and Lovers* in 1913 completed the break, especially in that Jessie Chambers was shocked and upset by the way in which she was portrayed as Miriam in the final version of the novel, and she never spoke or wrote to Lawrence again after reading the proof-sheets. It is possible too that she had been upset by the news of Lawrence's elopement for it seems likely (and understandable) that she had expected him to marry her. In any case Lawrence had cut himself off from his past life, and with Frieda he settled down to work as an author by beginning a new novel, first called *The Sisters*, which title was later to become *The Wedding Ring* before finally being published as two novels, *The Rainbow* and *Women in Love*.

Lawrence and Frieda spent a good part of the time between 1912 and 1914 in Italy and Germany, but they were in England at the outbreak of the First World War and were forced to remain in the country until 1919. Lawrence's attitude to the war, certainly not unjustifiably, was completely hostile and he attempted to isolate himself from it, not out of an unrealistic desire to avoid unpleasant facts of existence but because of his contempt for the issues on which the war was fought and for its effects on great masses of people. This feeling of contempt is difficult to rationalise into any neat formula, but it is important to remember that his objections were not specifically political, and his position was in no way similar to that of the many conscientious objectors who were imprisoned for their beliefs at the time. It is worth noting that Bertrand Russell, who was eventually imprisoned for refusing to fight, was involved with Lawrence in a series of lectures objecting to the war, but soon Russell was forced to break off the friendship. 'it was only gradually that we discovered that we differed from each other more than either differed from the Kaiser', as Russell later commented. Lawrence was medically unfit for military service and never had to plead his case before a court. In 'The Nightmare' chapter (XII) of *Kangaroo* Lawrence sets out his own feelings about the war in an extreme form through the character of Somers:

> From 1916 to 1919 a wave of criminal lust rose and possessed England, there was a reign of terror, under a set of indecent bullies like Bottomley of *John Bull* and other bottom-dog members of the House of Commons. Then Somers had known what it was to live in a perpetual state of semi-fear: the fear of the criminal public and the criminal government. . . .
>
> Many men, carried on a wave of patriotism and true belief in democracy, entered the war. Many men were driven in out of belief that it was necessary to save their property. Vast numbers of men were just bullied into the army. A few remained. Of these, many became conscientious objectors.
>
> Somers tiresomely belonged to no group. He would not enter the army, because his profoundest instinct was against it. Yet he had no conscientious objection to war. It was the whole spirit of the war, the vast mob-spirit, which he could never acquiesce in. The terrible, terrible war, made so fearful because in every country practically every man lost his head, and lost his own centrality, his own manly isolation in his own integrity, which alone keeps life real. Practically every man being caught away from himself, as in some horrible flood and swept away with the ghastly masses of other men, utterly unable to speak, or feel for himself, or to stand on his own feet, delivered over and swirling in the current, suffocated for the time being. Some of them to die for ever. pp. 215–16

This is hardly one of the great arguments against war, but the reader should not be too hasty in condemning Lawrence's position so far as it is discernible because of the uncontrolled effusiveness of the prose. Another picture of Lawrence at the time is given by Lady Cynthia Asquith, who gives a more balanced account of the effect of the war on him:

> About a year after my first meeting with Lawrence the war of 1914–1919 began. I had a letter from him in which he wrote, 'The outbreak of war finished me, it was the spear through the side of all sorrows and hopes.'
>
> When I next saw him he really was visibly changed. At times he looked like one in acute physical pain. He spoke of the war as a

'colossal and deliberate horror. Gusts of rage alternated with bitter grief. 'My soul is fizzling savagely,' he hissed, 'it is sending me MAD.' And, in truth, ever afterwards he did seem to me to have, though of course with radiant lucid intervals, a touch of delirium— to talk and write like one whose temperature is several degrees above normal.

A passionate subjectivist, now more than ever at odds with the nightmare facts of an objective world that impinged upon him on every side, he was reduced to gnashing, impotent misery. To him the war was not only the immediate horror it was to all of us; he had the despair of prevision as well. Convinced as he was that one war must always breed another, he saw it as a suicide-pact between the nations, as the beginning of the end—in his own words, 'the end of democracy, the end of the idea of liberty and freedom, the end of the brotherhood of man, the end of the belief in the reign of love, the end of the belief that man desires peace, harmony, tranquillity, love and loving kindness. The end of Christianity . . . the end, the end. . . .'

Despite his loathing and denunciation of the war, Lawrence could not fail to recognise—and this fact obsessed him—that it did at least bring about what he called 'a slump in trifling,' and trifling was what he detested. But that human beings should find in war an inspiration and fulfilment nothing else seemed able to give them, that this should be so, was to him a confession of failure; a blasphemy that filled him with despair. Some other moral equivalent must be found; new values proclaimed; a wholly different idea of life conceived.   Cynthia Asquith, REMEMBER AND BE GLAD, p. 136

It is difficult to be objective even at this date about the war and Lawrence's attitude to it. However sane or inexcusable we may feel his stand to have been, conditions were made even more unpleasant for him in 1915 when *The Rainbow* was suppressed only a few weeks after its publication. The reasons for the ban are not clear: apparently at the time it was thought that the novel was objectionable because of certain sexual scenes (although it is difficult today to see what passages could be called in question by anyone) but it has since appeared more likely that publication of the book was stopped because of disparaging references to the fighting men as 'wooden soldiers'. Whatever the reason for its ridiculous suppression, the whole affair had a serious effect on Lawrence. As Martin Secker, who was later to publish his work, has recently commented: 'It is perhaps of significance that thereafter he was never again resident in England, and that his only visits to this country were of the briefest duration and at long intervals.'

AFTER THE WAR: 1919–1930

The suppression of *The Rainbow* hampered Lawrence in his attempt to have his next novel, *Women in Love*, published in England, although some of his other writings did appear, notably the travel book *Twilight in Italy* in 1916 and some verse including the volume *Look! We Have Come Through* in 1917 ('They may have come through, but why should we look?' asked Bertrand Russell). Lawrence left England in 1919 as soon as he was able to obtain a passport after the end of hostilities, and the last few years of his life were spent travelling abroad, first in Italy, and then on around the world through Ceylon, Australia, the United States and Mexico, and finally back to Europe. Only in Mexico was he able to establish any roots, but the security he found there was hampered by his growing ill-health, his uncertainty over his relationship with Frieda, and the continued persecution of censors who banned some of his work in England, the United States, and Australia.

Women in Love was published first in the United States in 1920, for as we have seen Lawrence found that it was impossible to publish it in England during the war. He wrote to the American poet Amy Lowell on 30 August 1917 that

> Nobody will publish my novel *Women in Love*—my best bit of work. The publishers say 'it is too strong for an English public.' Poor darling English public, when will it go in for a little spiritual athletics? Are those Tommies, so tough and brown on the outside, are they really so pappy and unbaked inside, that they would faint and fall under a mere dose of *Women in Love*?

Eventually the novel was published in England in the autumn of 1921, and was not suppressed in spite of a spirited public campaign to have it banned. Some of the arguments advanced by those who wished to censor the book read as quite utterly preposterous today. Under a headline

A BOOK THE POLICE SHOULD BAN
Loathsome Study of Sex Depravity—Misleading Youth
To Unspeakable Disaster

W. Charles Pilley was compelled to exclaim in *John Bull* on 17 September 1921 that 'I cannot sit idly by and see this neurotic production exposed for sale on the bookstalls as a 'novel'. It is nothing of the sort. It is a shameless study of sex depravity which in direct proportion to the skill of its literary execution becomes unmentionably vile.'

It is perhaps amusing for us today to recall ridiculous remarks of this sort made at the time, but of course it was not amusing for Lawrence to see one of the greatest novels of the century discussed in this way. It is easy to see a certain element of escapism in Lawrence's continual restless desire to move on and on around the world in his last eleven years—a tendency to avoid some of the unpleasant facets of life in the 1920s, which does perhaps betray an uneasiness as to the validity of some of his own attitudes of which Lawrence was himself aware in the portrait of Birkin in *Women in Love*. At the same time Lawrence's own rootlessness and dissatisfaction can surely be explained as being at least partly the result of the constant pillorying and vilifying of his character and books, with the resultant public image of him. Rhys Davies, who knew Lawrence in 1928 in the south of France, brings this out well:

> He was caged by censorship and persecution chiefly, but there was also his consumption [tuberculosis] and the exile this meant; and he was caged by the contempt, the laughter, the cheap sneers and the suggestive and cunning propaganda of his enemies who spoke and wrote of him at that time (*Lady Chatterley's Lover* had not long been published) as a frustrated sexual maniac, pornographic and indecent. Caged, which was the same thing as a retreat to the desert, he had arrived at that prophetic stage (and these were the last two years of his life) when the civilised human race appears one

day as effete idiots, another as a pack of hyenas and wolves. But though he writhed away, he could not turn his back on people, he could not rid himself of his vehement awareness of people: this was the motive power of his tremendous nervous vitality—and this it was that was treacherously exhausting his body. His condition at this period might have been called tragic.

HORIZON II, 10 (October 1940), p. 194

The outcry against *Women in Love* in England was as nothing compared with that raised by the publication of *Lady Chatterley's Lover* in 1928, and by the exhibition of Lawrence's paintings held in London in 1929, and most readers will be familiar with the censorship ban imposed on *Lady Chatterley's Lover* which was not lifted until the 1960s. The strange mixture of crazy humour and ludicrous tragedy of which these episodes are composed is far too complex to go into here, and the interested reader is strongly recommended to the relevant sections of the third volume of Nehls's *Composite Biography* (particularly Philip Trotter's description of the exhibition, pages 326–75). Lawrence was able to view the situation with humour as well as scorn, as is evidenced by a number of the poems of the period. ' "Gross, Coarse, Hideous" (Police Description of My Pictures)' (p. 680) contains an amusing aside at the guardians of public decency:

Lately I saw a sight most quaint:
London's lily-like policemen faint
in virgin outrage as they viewed
the nudity of a Lawrence nude.

One of the major complaints made by the legal authorities about the paintings was that Lawrence had given the nudes sexual organs and pubic hair, and had failed to clothe these regions with a fig-leaf or some other stray chance passing object, for, as the poem 'Innocent England' (p. 579) begins:

Oh what a pity, Oh! don't you agree
that figs aren't found in the land of the free.

Fig trees don't grow in my native land;
there's never a fig-leaf near at hand

21

when you want one; so I did without;
and that is what all the row's about.

Virginal, pure policemen came
and hid their faces for very shame,

while they carried the shameless things away
to gaol, to be hid from the light of day.

Even so, in spite of the humour, this sort of treatment by the authorities in England must have had a distressing effect on Lawrence's attitudes and on his health. He had never been healthy since catching pneumonia at the age of sixteen, and throughout the war he had been consistently rejected as unfit for military service even at the darkest times of the war when all available manpower was being conscripted. In 1929 Lawrence, infuriated by the treatment of his pictures and the continuing attacks on him because of *Lady Chatterley's Lover*, became seriously ill with tuberculosis, although he did not die until 2 March 1930 at Vence in the south of France, at the age of forty-four. Richard Aldington had written a little time before:

> People are so strangely unwilling to admit the genius of a living artist. They feel so meanly of themselves that they cannot believe that one of the gods is moving among *them*, that genius lives in *their* time. They are insulted by superiority and try to ignore it or to crush it. . . . But Lawrence gives you direct contact with his own mind and with the earth and with human life; and so—to our eternal shame—we call in the police-spies and the military and the lawyers and see to it that he is exasperated and hounded into exile and bitter rage. But then, of course, our moral indignation must be allowed to subside a little, for, after all, the Heretics always ask for what they get. Lawrence did go out of his way to dare the great British Bull, prodding it and snarling at it and flourishing little bits of red in its eyes; and he was more than a little surprised and scared when it charged him. So now he has to pretend that the Bull is about to expire of internal convulsions. I fear Lawrence will expire first. Yet such an old and haughty Bull, so proud in arms, ought to apologise because it was frightened by a poet. I think England owes Lawrence an apology. D. H. LAWRENCE, p. 42

2

Sex, Morality and the Novel

One of the major criticisms against D. H. Lawrence has been that his emphasis on sex is exaggerated and unrealistic, whilst he himself regarded a true understanding of it to be central to his work and the ideas on modern civilisation with which he was dealing. It is important, therefore, that any reader of his work should be aware of what Lawrence understood sex to be.

In discussing Lawrence's ideas in this chapter, however, it should be noted that he did not write in order to convey certain fixed moral ideas, on sex or anything else, but rather that the moral ideas emerge themselves from the imaginative and artistic experience of the writer in the act of creation. Lawrence's supposed didacticism has been sometimes overemphasised in the past, and although we do not have to accept completely his own statement at the beginning of his *Fantasia of the Unconscious* that

> This pseudo-philosophy—'pollyanalytics', as one of my respected critics might say—is deduced from the novels and poems, not the reverse. The novels and poems come unwatched out of one's pen. And then the absolute need which one has for some sort of satisfactory mental attitude towards oneself and things in general makes one try to abstract some definite conclusions from one's experiences as a writer and as a man. The novels and poems are pure passionate experience. These 'pollyanalytics' are inferences made afterwards from the experience.   Foreword, p. 9

there is more than an element of truth in it. Lawrence's ideas change and develop over the course of his writing career (part of their interest lies in tracing these changes) and he himself was violently opposed to taking up fixed moral positions.

Essentially, Lawrence's insistence on sex is a moral insistence on the need for an awareness of the possibilities of life. The moral basis of his view of sex is important, for sex to Lawrence is conceived as being closer to the traditional Christian view of marriage than it is to modern concepts of free love, promiscuity, or the activities of Don Juan or Casanova. His attitude to promiscuity, for example, is amusingly brought out in the poem 'In a Spanish Tram-car':

> She fanned herself with a violet fan
> and looked sulky, under the thick straight brows.

> The wisp of modern black mantilla
> made her half Madonna, half Astarte.

> Suddenly her yellow-brown eyes looked with a flare into mine;
> —we could sin together!—

> The spark fell and kindled instantly on my blood,
> then died out almost as swiftly.

> She can keep her sin
> She can sin with some thick-set Spaniard.
> Sin doesn't interest me.

Throughout his life Lawrence remained 'puritanical' in his attitude towards the unconventional sexual behaviour of many of the younger generation, particularly after the war, but his puritanism always involved a respect for life and a disgust for cheap exploitation of sex. He would have agreed with the Russian writer V. V. Rozanov's remark, which at first might seem almost blasphemous, that 'the relation of sex to God is stronger than the relation of intellect to God—stronger even than the relation of conscience to God'. This concept is a religious one, and to Lawrence sex was almost a religious activity. This is brought out well in the essay 'Apropos of *Lady Chatterley's Lover*' which Lawrence wrote late in his life as an explanation of his most controversial novel (the essay is printed as a preface to the Heinemann Phoenix unexpurgated edition of *Lady Chatterley's Lover*):

Augustine said that God created the universe new every day: and to the living, emotional soul, this is true. Every dawn dawns upon an entirely new universe, every Easter lights up an entirely new glory of a new world opening in utterly new flower. And the soul of man and the soul of woman is new in the same way, with the infinite delight of life and the evernewness of life. So a man and a woman are new to one another throughout a life-time, in the rhythm of marriage that matches the rhythm of the year.

Sex is the balance of male and female in the universe, the attraction, the repulsion, the transit of neutrality, the new attraction, the new repulsion, always different, always new. The long neuter spell of Lent, when the blood is low, and the delight of the Easter kiss, the sexual revel of spring, the passion of midsummer, the slow recoil, revolt, and grief of autumn, greyness again, then the sharp stimulus of winter of the long nights. Sex goes through the rhythm of the year, in man and woman, ceaselessly changing: the rhythm of the sun in his relation to the earth. Oh, what a catastrophe for man when he cut himself off from the rhythm of the year, from his unison with the sun and the earth. Oh, what a catastrophe, what a maiming of love when it was made a personal, merely personal feeling, taken away from the rising and the setting of the sun, and cut off from the magic connection of the solstice and the equinox! This is what is the matter with us. We are bleeding at the roots, because we are cut off from the earth and sun and stars, and love is a grinning mockery, because, poor blossom, we plucked it from its stem on the tree of Life, and expected it to keep on blooming in our civilised vase on the table.   pp. 29–30

Sex to Lawrence was important because it was the only chance civilised man had of remaining in contact with the greater universe of nature and hence of reality, but modern industrial civilisation had perverted man and perverted sex. Lawrence's view was that this perversion had resulted in a split between thought and feeling, so that men became dominated by their minds and made no effort to recreate the two in harmony. True moral awareness of life was only possible when thought and feelings were united in the whole man, and it was to this end that his novels were written. As he said elsewhere in the essay 'Apropos of Lady Chatterley's Lover':

In fact, thought and action, word and deed, are two separate lives which we lead. We need, very sincerely, to keep a connection. But while we think we do not act, and while we act we do not think. The great necessity is that we should act according to our thoughts, and think according to our acts. But while we are in thought we cannot really act, and while we are in action we cannot really think. The two conditions, of thought and action, are mutually exclusive. Yet they should be recreated in harmony.

And this is the real point of this book. I want men to be able to think sex, fully, completely, honestly and cleanly.

This effectively gives the lie to the notion that Lawrence's concern was solely with the primitive and uncivilised. Sex in Lawrence is not merely an end in itself, not merely an entertainment or a means of producing children, but a means towards determining reality, and this 'reality' is seen as existing in the immediate world of nature. Lawrence's philosophy is basically naturalistic, and the superb evocations of a sense of the fullness of life in his natural descriptions of places and things are what make his work so immediately appealing. To be alive in the flesh is magnificent, and sexual fulfilment is the awareness of this life in oneself and the world outside. The world of nature is conceived as supplying meaning to existence, as an antithesis to the diseased world of man in society.

This idea is, of course, a development of a Romantic view about nature which was essentially a 19th-century phenomenon, and it is worth noting in this respect that Lawrence's ideas are within a definite European moral tradition which includes such figures as Rousseau and Tolstoy, and are not merely the distorted and peculiar aberrations of one man. Lawrence's position in the history of ideas is, in fact, too often simply regarded as a modern variation of the 'back to nature' and 'noble savage' theorising of the previous century or so, as though he was in some way a 'modern Rousseau'. Certainly there are grounds for such an assessment, but an uncritical acceptance of it can easily mislead a reader into the assumption that he was some sort of 'noble savage' himself, that he was an 'emotional' rather than an 'intelligent' writer, and that his continued insistence on sex precludes any real regard for the intellect.

The whole question of Lawrence's intelligence has been complicated unnecessarily by the widespread currency of T. S. Eliot's remark in *After Strange Gods* that Lawrence has 'an incapacity for what we ordinarily call thinking'—a statement which on close examination may well mean little more than saying that Lawrence doesn't 'think' in the way that T. S. Eliot does. It is true, as we shall see, that Lawrence believed it to be a matter of the utmost vital urgency that 20th-century man should accept his physical and animal nature, and as he wrote in 1913 in a letter to Ernest Collings on 17 January:

> my great religion is a belief in the blood, the flesh as wiser than the intellect. We can go wrong in our minds. But what our blood feels and believes and says is always true.

Yet it must be constantly stressed that he is far from being a prophet of animalism pure and simple, and there is no conflict in Lawrence's work between flesh and real spirit or real intellect. Flesh and spirit, body and intellect should all be parts of man, but an undue emphasis on one to the exclusion of the other is crippling to man's whole moral and psychological well-being, and Lawrence's attack was never at the essence of the intellect itself but at the undue importance given to it in modern society and to its numerous sham counterfeits. 'Be a good animal, true to your animal instinct' may have been Annable's motto in *The White Peacock* but, as the narrator goes on to add, 'with all this, he was fundamentally very unhappy—and he made me also wretched'.

The general outline of these views, of course, will suggest that they are not entirely original to Lawrence. His attitude of rebellion to the values of contemporary society, and his overall moral concern, arise essentially from a contact with nature and the natural world. He writes in a tradition which reacted violently against the ordered and reasonable and ultimately meaningless world view, which Rousseau saw reflected in 18th-century optimism, Tolstoy in the upper-class social world of Tsarist

Russia, and Lawrence himself in industrialised 20th-century England. In the work of these writers there is a marked belief that man is and must remain part of nature, and that the more 'natural' man is then the better he is. Nature is right, and in so far as it is to be followed, man's animal nature is a good and admirable quality. Lawrence develops this idea to its logical conclusion, making sexual relationships the basis of his naturalistic viewpoint, for in a world dominated by the huge excesses of industrial society, sex is the only remaining link with nature.

It may be that Lawrence's ideas were misguided in some respects, and that, as many critics have complained, they do have unfortunate or even disastrous consequences. What cannot be denied, however, is the seriousness and urgency which always overrides the occasional confusion of the ideas, and one's overpowering impression of them is of a genuine attempt to deal with life honestly, without any falsification. Lawrence's remark in a letter to Edward Garnett of 18 April 1913 that

> I can only write what I feel pretty strongly about: and that, at present, is the relation between men and women. After all, it is *the* problem today, the establishment of a new relation, or the readjustment of the old one, between men and women.
>
> MOORE LETTERS, I, p. 200

may well strike some readers as needing considerable qualification (was it really *the* problem in 1913, important as it was?), but for good or ill the fact that he felt it to be of importance is indisputable. And, indeed, the over-romanticised and glamorous importance which our century gives to love and sex, and the problems which we have made for ourselves as a result of our dismissal of traditional values towards these, should at least give Lawrence's opinions some interest. Lawrence's wish to establish 'a new relation . . . between men and women' directly challenges the concept of romantic love as it is still presented to us incessantly through the commercial media of the cinema, pop-songs and advertising. To Lawrence this elevation of 'love' as the be-all and end-all of existence is entirely deplorable, for as it is presented to us it is sham and spurious; the 'love' of the pop-songs is often nothing more than a desire for security, for some certainty in a dark and alien world that 'somebody out there loves me', whereas the whole point of a proper sexual relationship is to make one aware of new possibilities and depth of life, and to bring one closer to an understanding of the reality underlying existence.

MORALITY AND THE NOVEL

In his work Lawrence is concerned about certain ideas and values, but, as it has been already suggested in this chapter, these values are not to be regarded as part of a fixed or absolute doctrine which he is claiming as valid for all people at all times. He sees sex as the particular problem of the 20th century, and where he and his characters are concerned it is essentially through sexual relationships of a particular kind that fulfilment in life can be obtained, but he would refuse to accept that these are universal laws for all men. It is worth repeating too that the ideas and values with which Lawrence is dealing in his novels emerge *from* the artistic experience of the writer rather than that they are grafted *on to* the artistic experience: the novels are not written simply in order to convey certain ideas about life, but to see whether the ideas can stand up to the experiences of the characters. Lawrence held that the novel was the ideal medium for discussing and examining the validity of moral ideas, for the novelist can show these ideas in action, affecting the lives of his characters and changing them for good or ill. The novelist's function is essentially to convey a realistic impression of life, for in a good novel everything happens as it has to happen as a logical development of character and plot. If the ideas which are affecting a character's life are false or spurious they will be seen to be so within the world of the novel, or the novelist will be forced to make his characters act in an unrealistic way so that the reader will inevitably see through them.

The point can perhaps be better grasped if we remember that good novelists are not always aware from the start of the way in which their plots and characters are going to develop. They start with a character or group of characters in a certain situation and allow the story to develop 'naturally' or 'realistically' from that point—'the novels and stories come unwatched out of one's pen'. Pushkin is said to have commented about his heroine whilst writing his poetic novel *Eugene Onegin* that 'my Tatiana has gone and got married—I should never have thought it of her', and Tolstoy and Dickens are examples of very different novelists who often began their novels without any clear idea of where and how they would end. In Lawrence's case many of the novels are allowed to develop themselves towards unknown ends, and in his work, as we shall see, the ideas with which he begins are modified or developed by the time the book comes to an end into larger problems which cannot be properly resolved in the one novel and have to be carried on into the next one, which often accounts for their 'plotless' quality and the relative weakness of some of their endings. It is true of course that the novelist must exercise some control over what is happening, but in Lawrence's case this 'control' is seen as illuminating the moral ideas which are emerging rather than in forcing these on to the story. Lawrence does in fact spend considerable time and effort in revising his major novels before the published version—there are usually three drafts of each novel, and each new draft involves a major revision of the previous one (a fact which those who persist in regarding Lawrence as an undisciplined and over-emotional writer might well remember) —but this revision does not entail, in theory at least, allowing the didactic aim to triumph over the artistic design. No great novel is written for the purpose of demonstrating an idea; a moral theme, if it is to emerge at all, must emerge naturally from the interpenetration of plot and character and not be forced on to the plot.

LAWRENCE AS A TECHNICAL INNOVATOR: SYMBOLISM AND IMAGERY

Lawrence held strong views on the suitability of the novel-form as a means of dealing with the ideas which concerned him, as is evidenced by the important essays 'Why the Novel Matters' and 'Morality and the Novel', in which he claims the novel to be a better vehicle for discussing moral ideas than even philosophy, religion or science. At the same time he was aware of the particular problems the novelist faced who wished to convey certain issues in an artistic and readable way, and although he certainly does not always avoid a tendency towards 'preaching' at the reader, he is able, by means of the use of symbolism, to discuss complex issues in an amazing artistic fashion.

Few critics in the past have given Lawrence the credit he deserves as a technical innovator, for the illusion has been widespread that as a writer he is usually too emotional and unrestrained to concern himself with technical problems of order and form. In spite of the care with which the major novels are known to have been written, of his original and individual interpretation of the function of character in the novel, and of the superb insights in his criticism of Russian, French and English novelists, the assumption has too glibly been made that Lawrence writes loosely and that his best writing is in some way accidental and unplanned—the 'wild, untutored phoenix' writing brilliantly at times in spite of himself. In fact, Lawrence is conscious heir to the two very separate traditions of the American and Russian novel as well as to the English tradition, and he is the first modern English writer of note to be so largely influenced by the great work of Tolstoy and Dostoevsky, Melville and Hawthorne. Good English translations of the Russian novelists began to appear at the beginning of the century and had an immediate impact, yet before the publication of the work of Tolstoy and Dostoevsky in England, and even in spite of the work of Henry James and Conrad, the novel had generally been regarded as an inferior form of literature, not fit to rank with history, philosophy, or even poetry as a medium for expressing serious ideas. At the end of the 19th century Hardy had been forced to give up writing novels after the outcry over *Jude the Obscure* because he felt that he could not deal honestly with themes that were important to him, in that neither the public nor publishers were prepared to accept the implications of what he wanted to say or admit his right to say it.

Lawrence, it is well known, did not find the English public any more tolerant than Hardy had done, but at least Lawrence had examples before him illustrating that moral ideas could be discussed in the novel at a supreme level of artistry and could

31

learn from the Russian novelists in particular how this could best be done. At the same time Lawrence develops these features in his own way: his novels read meaningfully at the purely realistic level of what his characters say and do, but a good deal of their significance can only be understood by realising that they also exist at another level. In the major novels (*Sons and Lovers*, *The Rainbow*, and *Women in Love*) the full meaning and much of the superb artistry derives from the symbolic use of imagery which the reader needs to note. The flower imagery in *Sons and Lovers*, for example, which will be more fully discussed in the next chapter, is not included simply for its picturesque appeal, but for the light it throws on certain characters and scenes. Similarly in *The Rainbow* the repetition of the images of arches and rainbows which recur throughout the novel have a more than incidental significance, and so does the moon image which occurs in several important episodes in that book and in *Women in Love*. More attention will be paid to these features in succeeding chapters; here it is enough to point out the existence of this device and its importance in any understanding of Lawrence's real genius as a writer. Lawrence has a magnificent gift for natural description, but these descriptions are not included simply as background, for they often contain much of the point, in a symbolic sense, of the episodes in which they occur.

The fact that Lawrence's major novels must be read at these two levels of realism and symbolism, of course, does not in itself mark him out as an original technical innovator in the novel. Other previous novelists had used imagery and symbolism to point their theme, but in Lawrence's case imagery is not used simply as a secondary means of elucidation of the basic plot. In his best work the two levels of realism and symbolism are equally important and a *balance* is struck between them. In terms of character, for example, the character is himself on the level of the main realistic plot, but he often equally importantly represents certain concepts. Early in *Women in Love* the two sisters, Ursula and Gudrun, see Gerald Crich as they wait at the railway level-crossing:

> Whilst the two girls waited, Gerald Crich trotted up on a red Arab mare. He rode well and softly, pleased with the delicate

quivering of the creature between his knees. And he was very picturesque, at least in Gudrun's eyes, sitting soft and close on the slender red mare, whose long tail flowed on the air. He saluted the two girls, and drew up at the crossing to wait for the gate, looking down the railway for the approaching train. In spite of her ironic smile at his picturesqueness, Gudrun liked to look at him. He was well-set and easy, his face with its warm tan showed up his whitish, coarse moustache, and his blue eyes were full of sharp light as he watched the distance.

The locomotive chuffed slowly between the banks, hidden. The mare did not like it. She began to wince away, as if hurt by the unknown noise. But Gerald pulled her back and held her head to the gate. The sharp blasts of the chuffing engine broke with more and more force on her. The repeated sharp blows of unknown, terrifying noise struck through her till she was rocking with terror. She recoiled like a spring let go. But a glistening, half-smiling look came into Gerald's face. He brought her back again, inevitably.

The noise was released, the little locomotive with her clanking steel connecting-rod emerged on the highroad, clanking sharply. The mare rebounded like a drop of water from hot iron. Ursula and Gudrun pressed back into the hedge, in fear. But Gerald was heavy on the mare, and forced her back. It seemed as if he sank into her magnetically, and could thrust her back against herself.

'The fool!' cried Ursula loudly. 'Why doesn't he ride away till it's gone by?'

Gudrun was looking at him with black-dilated, spellbound eyes. But he sat glistening and obstinate, forcing the wheeling mare, which spun and swerved like a wind, and yet could not get out of the grasp of his will, nor escape from the mad clamour of terror that resounded through her, as the trucks thumped slowly, heavily, horrifyingly, one after the other, one pursuing the other, over the rails of the crossing.   pp. 102–3

In itself this seems a simple enough episode, but its real function lies on a symbolic level in showing what Gerald Crich is and what he represents. There is no need for him to keep the horse close to the train at the crossing, but in doing it his attitude to nature is brought out in some depth and with considerable force. One feature of Lawrence's symbolism is its complexity, and it is facile to attempt to explain scenes such as these in terms of equations, but largely his desire to dominate and master the horse is really a desire to dominate nature, to force it under his control. At the same time this desire is shown as being ridiculous, in that there is no point in his doing so, but in this he is fulfilling his function within the novel. He is not only an industrialist, but he also represents the modern world of industry and science: he is it, and he is important to our understanding of the novel in that he exists both as a person and a concept, and that there is a balance between them. He is both things, equally.

It is the idea of balance which is important, for many authors have characters who, to put it naïvely, 'stand for' certain ideas. Shakespeare obviously is one example, where Cordelia in *King Lear* represents charity, mercy, understanding, in much the same way as the heroines of the last plays, Imogen, Perdita, Marina, symbolise the virtues of love and regeneration. In these cases, however, what these characters *stand for* is more important than what they are as *people* on a realistic level. The novelist, however, has to preserve the 'realism' of the characters at all costs, or else the reader ceases to believe in the importance of what he is reading about. Jane Austen is another example of an author who uses characters to represent certain concepts of pride and prejudice, sense and sensibility, but her characters are essentially people first and are representative of these ideas secondarily. Moreover, compared with Lawrence, her use of this other 'symbolic' level is sparing and restrained, whereas in Lawrence the symbolic level is, in *The Rainbow* and *Women in Love* at least, as important as the realistic one.

Lawrence's technical innovation in developing his novels on the two related levels of realism and symbolism is his great artistic achievement, and gives his work the aesthetic force and appeal which a more straight-forwardly didactic author would lack. As a technical innovator he is not as great in the history of the English novel as Henry James, nor so obviously experimental and revolutionary as Joyce, but what he does has particular relevance for the sort of novel he was writing and enables him convincingly to discuss certain moral issues in some depth at a superb level of artistry, as we shall see.

34

3

The Early Novels to *Sons and Lovers*

Lawrence's major novels were published in the following order:

The White Peacock	1911
The Trespasser	1912
Sons and Lovers	1913
The Rainbow	1915
Women in Love	1920
The Lost Girl	1920
Aaron's Rod	1922
Kangaroo	1923
The Plumed Serpent	1926
Lady Chatterley's Lover	1928

His work can best be understood by following the development of the themes and ideas which occur in the novels, and where the major books are concerned there is point in reading them in the order in which they were written so as to see how the issues dealt with are developed. Yet it is not advisable for a reader entirely new to Lawrence's work to begin by reading either of the two early novels, *The White Peacock* or *The Trespasser*, for although both have a certain charm and appeal they cannot be recommended as the best introduction to his writing. Both works are obviously written before Lawrence found his real capabilities as a writer, and their very real virtues are outweighed by stylistic weaknesses not to be found in Lawrence's third book, *Sons and Lovers*, which is one of the great novels of our literature.

'THE WHITE PEACOCK'

The main fault of Lawrence's first novel, *The White Peacock* (which was written over a period of four years from 1906–1910 and was published in 1911), lies in its over-idyllic element of wish-fulfilment. The name of the central family in it—the Beardsalls—indicates this element clearly, for Beardsall was his mother's maiden name, and the novel obviously deals with the sort of life Lawrence felt he might have had if his mother had had money and been able to leave his father early in their marriage and bring her children up in a wholly rural and middle-class way of life. In the novel the father appears briefly early on, but soon dies so that he does not corrupt the idyllic and unrealistic world with which the novel deals. The plot revolves around Lettie Beardsall, the sister of the narrator and the 'peacock' of the title, and her relationships with George Saxton, a young farmer whom she finds physically attractive, and with Leslie Tempest, son of the local leading family and representative of those middle-class virtues which she desires, and whom she marries, to George Saxton's anguish and undoing.

The themes of the novel are typical of those class relationships which Lawrence was to handle so much more successfully in his later work, but it would be wrong to write the novel off entirely as a failure. The book has faults, for the style is too 'literary' and forced and is obviously too much of its period in its combination of late 19th-century aestheticism (George Saxton is spurred on to make another attempt to win Lettie at one point by seeing reproductions of Aubrey Beardsley's illustrations) and slightly over-romanticised depiction of nature which recalls the work of the 'Georgian' poets (such as John Masefield, W. H. Davies, and early Rupert Brooke) which was then just coming into favour. Mention of 'Georgian' poetry, however, enables us to see by comparison that even in this early work Lawrence's ability to describe the natural world of the Nottingham countryside is much more vivid and compelling than Georgian descriptions of nature, which Kenneth Allot has wittily summed up as 'the characteristic insipidities of the Georgian poets with their cult of respectability and their pastoral week-end England of trout streams, parish churches, cricket, and R.S.P.C.A. collecting-boxes'. Whatever we may think of Lawrence's style in the novel at least his depiction of nature is the result of real and detailed observation.

Lawrence's treatment of nature in *The White Peacock* is of further interest in relation to the character of the gamekeeper, Annable. On the whole the character portrayal in the novel is weak and unconvincing, but in Annable Lawrence briefly indicates some of the features which were to make his later work so powerful, and the character of the gamekeeper needs to be borne in mind when any assessment of Lawrence's 'animalism' is discussed. Annable revels in his 'animal' nature, but the life that he lives is neither admirable nor satisfying. His home life is lived in squalor, his present wife is treated simply as a beast of burden to cater for his 'natural' animal needs of food and sex. He delights more in the senseless cruelty of nature around him than in its beauty, and for the short time he plays a part in the novel he throws a shadow over the idyll of romance which occupies the lives of the other characters. It is true that he is too complex a character for Lawrence to handle properly at this early stage, but he is a prototype of what is to come and a figure which any writer with Lawrence's interest needs to take into account. At times he is almost a character out of Jacobean tragicomedy with his disgust at humanity: 'He was a man of one idea:— that all civilisation was the painted fungus of rottenness. . . . He hated any sign of culture. When he thought, he reflected on the decay of mankind—the decline of the human race into folly and weakness and rottenness' (pp. 145–6). As a figure out of Jacobean drama he is out of place in the world of *The White Peacock*, indeed, Lawrence seems to have changed his mind about Annable's role during the course of the novel, for the issue his presence raises is touched on only in passing before he is killed mid-way through the book. His hatred of humanity and more particularly of women ('all vanity and screech and defilement') is explained somewhat unconvincingly by his past life, for he came of a good-class family, went to Cambridge, and became a parson before marrying into the aristocracy. This existence he found unbearable and he left his wife and disappeared, before taking up the very different life of a gamekeeper. Lawrence fails to fit this story adequately into the plot of the novel, but the class problems it raises become of more importance in the later novels, and Annable's history is obviously similar to that of Mellors in *Lady Chatterley's Lover*. Perhaps the most important thing to remember about *The White Peacock* is that Annable is not Lawrence, nor does he have Lawrence's approval, although he certainly possesses his interest.

'THE TRESPASSER'

The Trespasser was written between 1910 and 1912, and is based upon an unfortunate love affair between Helen Corke, who was a close friend of Lawrence's whilst he was teaching at Croydon, and her violin teacher, H. B. MacCartney. The plot of the novel is a simple one, describing the experiences of the music-teacher, Siegmund, and Helena, who spend a few days together on the Isle of Wight before Siegmund returns to his wife and family in the south of London. For reasons which can only be set out clearly in the novel itself, Siegmund commits suicide a few days after his return.

Like *The White Peacock*, *The Trespasser* has many awkward stylistic features which relate it very much to its time (both Siegmund and Helena refer to their fathers as 'pater'), but it has virtues in its descriptions of natural scenery and, more importantly, in its analysis of the love relationship and in the character of Helena. Even at this early stage of his career (Lawrence was only twenty-three when the novel was published) it is clear that Lawrence had a remarkable ability for describing sexual relationships. The romantic element in the affair is handled sensitively and does not become overtly sentimental: the two are lovers, but they are also individuals, and it is because of the fact that both Siegmund and Helena are convincingly drawn that the novel is able to carry the reader's interest. Siegmund is weighed down by the deadness of his marriage to Beatrice, and sees in Helena the chance of escape into a more meaningful world, but neither can or will face up to the responsibilities which their love entails. Helena in particular wishes to see their relationship simply in terms of their few days together and not to look beyond these. Moreover, she is a character in the tradition of Miriam in *Sons and Lovers* who reacts away from too gross a contact with the physical side of love:

38

She belonged to that class of 'dreaming women' with whom
passion exhausts itself at the mouth. Her desire was accomplished
in a real kiss. . . . However, to the real man she was very cruel. . . .
For centuries a certain type of woman has been rejecting the 'animal' in humanity, till now her dreams are abstract, and full of
fantasy, and her blood runs in bondage, and her kindness is full of
cruelty.   p. 23

Helena's rejection, and his family's rejection of him when he
returns to his wife, set Siegmund on a path of despair which ends
in his suicide.

'SONS AND LOVERS'

The first point to note about *Sons and Lovers* is that it is a novel
and ought primarily to be read as such, for although it has
considerable interest both as an autobiography and as a psychological case-book its real virtue is as imaginative literature. Any
reader familiar with Lawrence's early life will be able to recognise
the similarity of Paul Morel's experiences in at least the first part
of the book with Lawrence's own, and of course the feature which
most distinguishes *Sons and Lovers* from the two previous novels
is the quality of actual, felt life which characterises the narration
in its depiction of the working-class background. There is virtually no suggestion in it of the idyllic and unreal world of *The
White Peacock*, and it is immediately clear to the reader that in
Sons and Lovers Lawrence is writing about life as he knew it, and
not as he might have wished it to be. It is clear also that from a
purely biographical point of view it is a novel which Lawrence
had to write for his own psychological well-being, and that the
classic Freudian situation of the Oedipus complex, of love of and
domination by the mother and hatred of the father, was essentially Lawrence's problem as it was Paul Morel's. *Sons and Lovers*
is obviously based upon Lawrence's own life, but it is not simply
or accurately autobiographical, for the second half of the novel
particularly makes Paul Morel deliberately different from
Lawrence himself: Paul is an artist whilst Lawrence was primarily a writer; Paul works for some time in the surgical-
appliance manufacturer's factory in Nottingham whilst Lawrence

worked there only for three months when he was sixteen; the Clara episode, perhaps the least convincing in the book, is not very accurately based upon any one experience of Lawrence's; and the portrayal of Miriam may well not be a fair and truthful portrait of Lawrence's childhood sweetheart, Jessie Chambers.

It is well to stress this obvious point from the start of our discussion of the novel to prevent us from being side-tracked in the way in which some previous commentators have been into discussing it in terms which are not specifically literary or critical. For *Sons and Lovers* remains as one of the great novels of the 20th century; whether it is unfair to Jessie Chambers in suggesting that she was like Miriam is irrelevant, and its greatness as a novel is not centrally dependent upon its psychologically revealing delineation of Lawrence's Oedipus complex.

The plot of the novel is outwardly simple and straightforward, describing as it does the married life of the Morels, and particularly the childhood and adolescence of their second son, Paul, in his relationships with three women—his mother, his childhood sweetheart Miriam Leivers, and a later lover, Clara Dawes. Yet the book is much more than the simple family chronicle so beloved of English circulating libraries, for it gives a detailed analysis of a young man's emotional development at the turn of the last century at a level of insight which was revolutionary at the time it was published (in 1913) and which still has much point. Lawrence himself asserted that 'it is the tragedy of thousands of young men in England', and the novel offers something of enormous value to the young reader moving towards an adult experience of literature and life. Paul Morel is almost destroyed by the destructive and possessive 'love' of both his mother and Miriam, and the nature of his relationships with them is magnificently brought out by Lawrence; but their 'love' for him is not shown as being unattractive or unwanted. Both relationships are shown as being meaningful and desirable in part, and the tragedy of them, with Paul left almost emotionally derelict at the end of the book, lies in the fact that in spite of the advantages they give they do not contribute towards wholeness of life. Both his mother and Miriam wish to possess Paul in their own ways, and to see him as they wish him to be and not exactly as he is.

The Morels

Lawrence's bias in *Sons and Lovers*, of course, is obviously in favour of the mother in the conflicts which take place both between Paul's parents and between the mother and Miriam, but it is important to remember Lawrence's own critical dictum —to trust the tale, not the teller—when reading the novel. That is to say, the novelist may write with conscious intent to take up certain attitudes in his work whilst the process of imaginative creation in the writing of the book may in fact suggest other attitudes. This is borne out almost from the start of the novel, for example in the scene where Morel comes home late at night from the public house:

At half-past eleven her husband came. His cheeks were very red and very shiny above his black moustache. His head nodded slightly. He was pleased with himself.

'Oh! Oh! waitin' for me, lass? I've bin 'elpin' Anthony, an' what's think he's gen me? Nowt b'r a lousy hae'f-crown, an' that's ivry penny—'

'He thinks you've made the rest up in beer,' she said shortly.

'An' I 'aven't—that I 'aven't. You b'lieve me, I've 'ad very little this day, I have an' all.' His voice went tender. 'Here, an' I browt thee a bit o' brandysnap, an' a coconut for th' children.' He laid the gingerbread and the coconut, a hairy object, on the table. 'Nay, tha niver said thankyer for nowt i' thy life, did ter?'

As a compromise, she picked up the coconut and shook it, to see if it had any milk.

'It's a good 'un, you may back yer life o' that. I got it fra' Bill Hodgkisson. "Bill," I says, "tha non wants them three nuts, does ter? Arena ter for gi'ein' me one for my bit of a lad an' wench?" "I ham, Walter, my lad," 'e says; "ta'e which on 'em ter's a mind." An' so I took one, an' thanked 'im. I didn't like ter shake it afore 'is eyes, but 'e says, "Tha'd better ma'e sure it's a good un, Walt." An' so, yer see, I knowed it was. He's a nice chap, is Bill Hodgkisson, 'e's a nice chap!'

'A man will part with anything so long as he's drunk, and you're drunk along with him,' said Mrs. Morel.

'Eh, tha mucky little 'ussy, who's drunk, I sh'd like ter know?'
said Morel. He was extraordinarily pleased with himself, because
of his day's helping to wait in the Moon and Stars. He chattered on.

Mrs. Morel, very tired, and sick of his babble, went to bed as
quickly as possible, while he raked the fire.   p. 6–7

This is the first introduction of Morel into the action of the novel,
and in itself the quotation shows his warmth and delicacy contrasted with the graceless and hard conduct of his wife, whose
action in shaking the coconut to see if it is 'good' is unpleasant
and insulting. In its context, however, the reader cannot regard
the scene in this way, for Lawrence has already prejudiced us
against Morel in the preceding pages by his sympathy for Mrs.
Morel's situation. The scene is typical of Lawrence's own predi-
lection in the novel, for as H. M. Daleski has aptly commented:
'the weight of hostile comment which Lawrence directs against
Morel is balanced by the unconscious sympathy with which he is
presented dramatically while the overt celebration of Mrs. Morel
is challenged by the harshness of the character in action' (*The
Forked Flame*, p. 43). However, Lawrence himself suggests that
Morel is an awkward and unpleasant parent, although the failure
in the marriage is obviously as much the mother's fault as
the father's, and Morel's supposed failure as a husband and
father is suggested as being the dominant factor in driving
the mother into closer sympathy with her children, particularly
Paul.

Lawrence's bias in describing the family life of the Morels
does not interfere, however, with the skill with which it is
depicted in literary terms, and the tension in the family between
the parents is what gives the early part of *Sons and Lovers* its
power and interest. The scenes between the parents are charged
with dramatic force which Lawrence is able to convey with
brutal realism. The tragedy of their married life is the failure of
both of them to adapt to the very different background and
attitude of the other, so that once the initial sensual element has
palled they spend their lives in mutual recrimination. The mother,
Gertrude, comes from a middle-class family and is fascinated by
Walter Morel when she first meets him:

He was well set-up, erect, and very smart. He had wavy black hair that shone again, and a vigorous black beard that had never been shaved. His cheeks were ruddy, and his red, moist mouth was noticeable because he laughed so often and so heartily. . . . He was so full of colour and animation, his voice ran so easily into comic grotesque, he was so ready and so pleasant with everybody.   p. 9

She is opposite to him in many ways, and he in consequence interests her. After the first few months of marriage, however, they drift apart when she tries 'to open her heart seriously to him' and she fails in her efforts to 'improve' him until they become almost totally estranged. For all of Lawrence's sympathy, it is obvious that Mrs. Morel fails to adjust to the demands of her marriage and remains quite unable to see the values of the working-class environment in which she finds herself, remaining detached and alien to her surroundings and attempting to influence her children to feel as she does.

Paul and Miriam

At the same time it must be recognised that the better life which she wishes for her children is certainly not to be deplored, and the novel is able to strike a fine balance between the virtues of Mrs. Morel's idealism and those of the working-class life in which the story is set. Her idealism is not mere social snobbery, and Paul in particular is able to respond to the warmth and vitality of the world into which he is born despite the family discord. He does not become a snob, and although he does not respect his father he is not out of key with his father's world. It is a remarkable achievement of *Sons and Lovers* that it manages to avoid any suggestion of the facile and merely political and social features of class-consciousness which has beset and stifled so much of English life in this century. The pictures of working-class life in the early part of the book are wonderfully evocative of the feel of the mining village of Bestwood, of the life of the miners and the warmth of their dialect, of the games of the children:

> Annie and Paul and Arthur loved the winter evenings, when it was not wet. They stayed indoors till the colliers were all gone

home, till it was thick dark, and the street would be deserted. Then they tied their scarves round their necks, for they scorned overcoats, as all the colliers' children did, and went out. The entry was very dark, and at the end the whole great night opened out, in a hollow, with a little tangle of lights below where Minton pit lay, and another far away opposite for Selby. The farthest tiny lights seemed to stretch out the darkness for ever. The children looked anxiously down the road at the one lamp-post, which stood at the end of the field path. If the little, luminous space were deserted, the two boys felt genuine desolation. They stood with their hands in their pockets under the lamp, turning their backs on the night, quite miserable, watching the dark houses. Suddenly a pinafore under a short coat was seen, and a long-legged girl came flying up.

'Where's Billy Pillins an' your Annie an' Eddie Dakin?'

'I don't know.'

But it did not matter so much—there were three now. They set up a game round the lamp-post, till the others rushed up, yelling. Then the play went fast and furious.

There was only this one lamp-post. Behind was the great scoop of darkness, as if all the night were there. In front, another wide, dark way opened over the hill brow. Occasionally somebody came out of this way and went into the field down the path. In a dozen yards the night had swallowed them. The children played on.

pp. 76-7

Paul is able to benefit from the values both of his environment and of his mother, and even though his mother's love is eventually crippling through its very force its virtues must not be underestimated. From his birth it is clear that his mother lavishes affection upon him as a reaction against the guilt she feels at the failure of her marriage. In the second chapter, 'The Birth of Paul', Mrs. Morel takes the baby out into the late summer evening and, looking at him, feels 'in some far inner place of her soul, that she and her husband were guilty':

She no longer loved her husband; she had not wanted this child to come, and there it lay in her arms and pulled at her heart. She felt as if the navel string that had connected its frail little body with hers had not been broken. A wave of hot love went over her to the infant. She held it close to her face and breast. With all her force, with all her soul she would make up to it for having brought it into the world unloved. She would love it all the more now it was here; carry it in her love. Its clear, knowing eyes gave her pain and fear. Did it know all about her? When it lay under her heart, had it been listening then? Was there a reproach in the look? She felt the marrow melt in her bones, with fear and pain.   pp. 36–7

It is a mark of Lawrence's genius as a writer that even in this unsentimental age such writing does not seem false or over-emotional. The values which the mother feels here, and those which she gives to Paul as he grows up, are genuine ones in themselves, and it is the sincerity and the sanity of the portrait of Paul which prevent him from appearing as either a prig or a snob to the reader. Lawrence's ability in portraying Paul (largely as an autobiographical self-portrait) is all the more remarkable when we remember the failure of Thackeray in *Pendennis* and even of Dickens in *David Copperfield* to carry through the portraits of their central characters convincingly without making them appear stilted and priggish when they pass through adolescence and early manhood. *Sons and Lovers* achieves its success where these other novels fail largely because of Lawrence's genuine attempt to deal sincerely with the complex emotions his character experiences and not to be dissuaded from his task by any notions of what the reading public might or might not be expected to want his hero to be like.

The genuineness of Paul's experiences is borne out not only in his relations with his mother, but also in his love and friendship with Miriam, detailed in the second part of the novel, and just as the conflicts between the parents had given the first part of the book its impelling tension so the struggle between Mrs. Morel and Miriam over Paul dominates this section. Although Miriam lives with her parents on their farm she is the opposite of the stereotyped image of the practical, natural country-girl. At first she is reluctant to offer her friendship to Paul, for she lives in a dream-world of spirituality:

Everywhere was a Walter Scott heroine being loved by men with helmets or with plumes in their caps. She herself was something of a princess turned into a swine-girl in her own imagination. And she was afraid lest this boy, who, nevertheless, looked something like a Walter Scott hero, who could paint and speak French, and knew what algebra meant, and who went by train to Nottingham every day, might consider her simply as the swine-girl, unable to perceive the princess beneath; so she held aloof. p. 142

Soon, however, she responds to Paul, and together they enjoy a platonic relationship which is a major factor in his development. She encourages and applauds his intellectual and artistic interests, and the real value which they both place on these interests is well conveyed by Lawrence. Yet Miriam is still very limited in her attitudes, and Paul finds her constant tendency to spiritualise and etherialise life more and more frustrating as the novel progresses, although at first he is unable to explain his sense of frustration in sexual terms. Miriam's refusal to accept or tolerate the physical aspects of life—indeed, her fear of life—is brought out symbolically in Chapter VII, 'Lad-and-Girl Love'. When she shows him the swing in the cowshed, for example, Paul enthusiastically plays on it, but when it comes to her turn she is reluctant and afraid when Paul begins pushing her higher. Her fear and sense of shame in this episode obviously relate to something more than just fear of the swing, and are characteristic of her. Again, soon after this, Miriam's nature is illustrated when late one evening she insists on showing him a wild-rose bush she has discovered, for even this simple enough act has to be spiritualised into something more than a natural event: 'They were going to have a communion together—something that thrilled her, something holy.' When they reach the bush Paul is disquieted and pained by her attitude, for the natural beauty of the rose is not enough for her:

> She looked at her roses. They were white, some incurved and holy, others expanded in an ecstacy. The tree was dark as a shadow. She lifted her hand impulsively to the flowers; she went forward and touched them in worship.
> 'Let us go,' he said.
> There was a cool scent of ivory roses—a white, virgin scent.

46

Something made him feel anxious and imprisoned. The two walked in silence.

'Till Sunday,' he said quietly, and left her; and she walked home slowly, feeling her soul satisfied with the holiness of the night. He stumbled down the path. And as soon as he was out of the wood, in the free open meadow, where he could breathe, he started to run as fast as he could. It was like a delicious delirium in his veins.

p. 160

This is indicative of the whole relationship. Miriam gives much to Paul and encourages him in his painting in a way in which his mother was unable to do for all her interest, but there are whole areas of life which she cannot face. Even though she lives on a farm Miriam is unable to face up to the physical realities 'of the continual business of birth and of begetting which goes on upon every farm', and at first she influences Paul to feel the same: 'their intimacy went on in an utterly blanched and chaste fashion. It could never be mentioned that the mare was in foal' (p. 162).

It is Miriam's blindness to certain features of life which so antagonises Mrs. Morel towards her. Paul cannot at first understand his mother's dislike of Miriam, and indeed his mother cannot properly make it explicit herself. The two women are of obviously different temperaments, as is evidenced, for example, three or four pages after the rose-bush episode, where the mother becomes full of enthusiasm over some 'glories of the snow' which she finds in her garden. The 'joy', 'excitement', and the 'elation' which she shows when she discovers the flowers contrasts markedly with the cloying sentimentality of Miriam's attitude towards the wild-roses. Partly, of course, Mrs. Morel's dislike of Miriam is that of a possessive mother jealous of any rival, but that it is not entirely this factor alone is shown by Mrs. Morel's relative friendship towards Clara. The real cause of the antagonism lies in Miriam's 'spirituality', for by her refusal or inability to see Paul as a lover rather than as an intellectual or artistic 'companion' she is challenging Mrs. Morel on the only grounds in which the mother can hope to continue her dominant relationship with her son. Mrs. Morel is understandably hostile towards the girl who becomes the centre of her son's artistic life and whose main fulfilment seems to lie in 'mothering' or caring for his soul and mind.

Eventually Paul himself begins to feel imprisoned and stifled by the kind of 'love' which Miriam is offering him, and he attempts to alter Miriam by suggesting that they become lovers in a physical sense. This itself naturally fails, and soon after Miriam has reluctantly given herself to Paul he breaks off the relationship and becomes more closely involved with Clara. Even here, however, one of the remarkable features of the novel can be noted, for it is impossible for the reader to find fault entirely with Paul or with Miriam. We can see some justification in Miriam's sense of outrage when she is cast off, although there is a certain smugness and self-satisfaction in her view that Paul is simply sowing wild oats with Clara before he returns—a smugness which we partly want to see hurt. There is also justification in Paul's behaviour, however, and a feeling that he has no alternative but to behave as he does, and the fact that we feel this way pays tribute to Lawrence's ability in depicting character. The realism of the whole relationship—the sincerity with which it is portrayed—is its most compelling feature. It is patently life-like that Paul should have struggled through to his understanding of the need to reject Miriam in spite of what she has to offer him, just as it is life-like for him to continue to be entirely unsure as to whether he ought to marry Miriam or not, even until almost the close of the novel. But the reader is in no doubt that giving in to Miriam will be the spiritual death of Paul, and much of the last half of the book involves the tension between Paul's drift towards either death or life.

Clara

Miriam's 'spirituality' finally becomes intolerable to Paul, who sees the true nature of her character in yet another flower-episode in Chapter IX, 'Defeat of Miriam', where she shows him some daffodils, going on to her knees before them, and taking one, 'caressing it with her mouth and cheeks and brow'. Her enthusiasm for the daffodils is still cloying:

'Aren't they magnificent?' she murmured.

'Magnificent! it's a bit thick—they're pretty.'

She bowed again to her flowers at his censure of her praise. He watched her crouching, sipping the flowers with fervid kisses.

'Why must you be always fondling things?' he said irritably.

'But I love to touch them,' she replied, hurt.

'Can you never like things without clutching them as if you wanted to pull the heart out of them? Why don't you have a bit more restraint, or reserve, or something?'

She looked up at him full of pain, then continued slowly to stroke her lips against a ruffled flower. Their scent, as she smelled, it was so much kinder than he; it almost made her cry.

'You wheedle the soul out of things,' he said 'as if you were a beggar for love. Even the flowers, you have to fawn on them—'

Rhythmically, Miriam was swaying and stroking the flower with her mouth, inhaling the scent which ever after made her shudder as it came to her nostrils.

'You don't want to love—your eternal and abnormal craving is to be loved. You aren't positive, you're negative. You absorb, absorb, as if you must fill yourself up with love, because you've got a shortage somewhere.'

She was stunned by his cruelty, and did not hear. He had not the faintest notion of what he was saying. It was as if his fretted, tortured soul, run hot by thwarted passion, jetted off these sayings like sparks from electricity. She did not grasp anything he said. She only sat crouched beneath his cruelty and his hatred of her. She never realised in a flash. Over everything she brooded and brooded. p. 218

In contrast, Clara is willing to accept Paul as a lover, and she is much more practical and realistic about life than is Miriam. At the same time it must be admitted that in the sections of the novel in which she appears Lawrence is much less able to convey a sense of the richness and immediacy of life than elsewhere, which may well relate in some way to the fact that the Clara episode is not based exactly on any one experience in Lawrence's own life. Slight though it is, there is an evident sense of contrivance in the character of Clara as Miriam's opposite, but at least the relationship between her and Paul does make clear the fact that Lawrence is not suggesting that any sexual relationship is enough in itself to provide a sense of purpose to life. Clara herself, in spite of her surface sophistication and hardness, leads an empty existence away from her husband, and from the first this sense of emptiness colours the affair with Paul. In the scene where they become lovers in Chapter XII, 'Passion', the description of the background evokes the true nature of their relationship magnificently in typical Lawrentian fashion: 'On either side stood the elm-trees like pillars along a great aisle, arching over and making high up a roof from which the dead leaves fell. All was empty and silent and wet.' Lawrence's handling of pace and tempo in the novel is masterly, as we shall discuss later, but it is not out of place to notice here how the slowness of the action deliberately makes its own comment on the actions of the characters. Immediately after the sentences just quoted Clara 'stood on top of the stile, and he held both her hands. Laughing, she looked down into his eyes. Then she leaped. Her breast came against his; he held her, and covered her face with kisses', but the slow rhythm of the sentences and the natural description combine to prevent us reading the episode in terms of gay, young love. An air of melancholy is delicately but surely cast over the scene (the image of the cathedral implicit in the description of the trees aids the impression that there is something not right about the relationship) and the reader can notice for himself how the loneliness of the scene is constantly interpolated ('All was silent and deserted') with the physical description of their actions. It can also be noted how Lawrence also evokes a sense of the limitations of the relationship again through use of flower-symbolism in the red carnations he gives Clara before the walk. Afterwards:

> When she arose, he, looking on the ground all the time, saw suddenly sprinkled on the black wet beech-roots many scarlet carnation petals, like splashed drops of blood; and red, small splashes fell from her bosom, streaming down her dress to her feet.
> 'Your flowers are smashed. he said.   p. 311

Paul and Clara fail to find any lasting meaning in their love, and eventually Clara becomes reunited with her husband, Baxter Dawes, although the reconciliation itself is uncertainly handled by Lawrence and is the most contrived feature of the novel. In terms of the structure of the book, however, both Clara and Baxter Dawes have the effect of widening the action of the story and of suggesting certain parallels, particularly between the characters of Baxter and Paul's father. Clara had left her husband because of his insensitive and brutal treatment of her, but (somewhat artificially) Paul makes her aware of her own mistakes in the marriage, and his rather unlikely friendship with Baxter helps to bring them together and leaves Paul alone at the time of his mother's death.

Structure and Imagery

The overall structure of *Sons and Lovers* is worth some consideration for it is remarkable how Lawrence is able to sustain the reader's interest in Paul's development and hold the suspense. Partly this is due, as we have seen, to the sincerity and realism of Paul's portrayal, and initially in the first part of the book to the tension between the parents and then to our involvement in the issues which Paul has to face. As Paul grows into manhood the underlying issue becomes clearer: the novel works on a balance between Paul's 'drift towards death' or towards life, and the various kinds of 'love' which Paul is offered are each in themselves crippling and have to be overcome. By the time the Clara episode is reached the question has become more explicit, and the time which Lawrence takes in getting the reader through this section is partly the reason for a falling-off in the interest at this point. There is a weakness too in the fact, mentioned early in our discussion, that Lawrence cannot bring himself to recognise clearly the fact that the mother's love for Paul is as crippling as Miriam's; and thus the overall design of the novel is somewhat blurred. The confusion in Lawrence's mind is mirrored even at the end of the novel in Paul's own sense of deprivation and uncertainty after his mother's death. Symbolically it is clear that Paul's killing of his mother by giving her an overdose of morphia has a significance beyond the simple act of mercy-killing:

as both Anthony West and Graham Hough have explained, the killing represents a rejection of her and a desire to free himself irrevocably (the chapter is called 'The Release'). When he is alone, Clara having gone back to Baxter Dawes, he is lost in an alien and unreal world (the last chapter is entitled 'Derelict'). Even at this point, however, he is able to reject the possibility of marrying Miriam, but the novel seems to be ending on a pessimistic and despairing note when in the last few sentences he turns back towards life—in Mark Schorer's well-known words—'as nothing in his previous history persuades us that he could unfalteringly do'.

In fact, of course, there is almost his whole previous history, the greater part of *Sons and Lovers*, which praises life and convinces us that Paul could do this. Yet Mark Schorer's remark is valid in that Paul's final choice for life as against death is unprepared for properly in the last few pages of the novel and is a weakness in it. 'One sheds one's sicknesses in books, repeats and presents again one's emotions to be master of them', Lawrence once commented, and obviously the psychological issues at work in Lawrence's own mind when writing the close of *Sons and Lovers* were enormous; and although these cannot justify the conclusion artistically they do render the critic reluctant to make nice distinctions at these points. Although it is not perfect in its overall structure, the last pages of the novel make urgent and horrifying reading, and rush the reader on to the dénouement:

> That evening he got all the morphia pills there were, and took them downstairs. Carefully he crushed them to powder.
> 'What are you doing?' said Annie.
> 'I s'll put 'em in her night milk.'
> Then they both laughed together like two conspiring children. On top of all their horror flickered this little sanity.   p. 394

But the urgency is that of psychological rather than artistic meaning.

The weakness in the overall structure of *Sons and Lovers*, which is caused largely by Lawrence's confusion over the exact nature of the issues he is dealing with, is compensated for by the immediacy with which the issues are conveyed and by Lawrence's handling of the story and his use of symbolism. A good deal of the dramatic readability of the novel depends on these elements, particularly in Lawrence's control of the pace and tempo of the narration: the descriptions of the natural background, for example, are not simply introduced for their picturesque appeal, but have both dramatic and symbolic relevance. In the early chapters much use is made of the contrast between the beauty of the countryside and the violence of the Morels' family life. In the second chapter, 'The Birth of Paul, and Another Battle', for example, there are sudden changes of scene and pace which highlight the theme, and these changes (which may seem clumsy and almost off-hand on first reading) are in fact delicately organised and prepared for. The scene where Morel comes home from the pit and finds his wife talking to the local Congregational clergyman and forces him to feel his wet pit singlet switches suddenly to an idyllic episode where Mrs. Morel takes the baby Paul into the late summer evening and holds him out towards the red sunset in what is possibly a slightly over-obvious symbolic offering to life, then again suddenly moves back to the Morel household and the violent domestic argument in which Mrs. Morel goads her husband into throwing a cupboard drawer at her head. These changes of scene act upon each other, and heighten the intensity of the family discord.

There is no room here to analyse the whole novel in terms of the effectiveness of these changes in the pace of the narration: the reader should be aware of them in each particular episode and note the fine sense of control which Lawrence exemplifies in the whole overall rhythm of *Sons and Lovers*. This control is aided also by the recurring use of certain symbolic devices, particularly in the flower-symbolism of the novel which is well detailed by Mark Spilka in his chapter 'How to Pick Flowers' in *The Love Ethic of D. H. Lawrence*. Mention of the importance of some of these flower-sequences has already been made earlier, and there is no need to repeat here the fact that their importance is not simply pictorial, although it could well be that there is a certain artificiality and awkwardness in the contrived use of every flower to carry some symbolic overtones of meaning; the technique is not always as masterly in this novel as it is to be in the following novels and in the short stories.

This is to make a minor cavil at the aspect of *Sons and Lovers* which makes it so excellent a novel: the feeling of the immediacy and richness of the natural background and hence of life itself. The world of nature is shown as a living force, and although it does not in itself supply a meaning to existence as it does in the work of Tolstoy or Wordsworth, it does have vital importance, and the sense of its beauty and power pervades the book. Lawrence is wonderfully able to evoke what Gerard Manley Hopkins termed 'the dearest freshness deep down things' and it is this which affects Paul in his attempt to find meaning in his relationships with other people. The novel stands as Lawrence's first major achievement, and opens the way for a proper understanding of the importance of sexual relationships conceived as spontaneous and liberating experiences. Paul Morel, like Lawrence himself, sees the need to relate sex to the freshness of the world of nature which surrounds man and not to regard it in its proper form as degrading, as he tries to tell Miriam:

> 'Don't you think we have been too fierce in our what they call purity? Don't you think that to be so much afraid and averse is a sort of dirtiness?' p. 281

Lawrence's next two novels develop this theme with magnificent power.

4

The Rainbow and *Women in Love*

[Lawrence's great virtue as a writer lies in his ability to evoke the richness of life and of nature and the way he relates this sense of richness to a viable code of human behaviour through an analysis of sexual relationships] it is in *The Rainbow* and *Women in Love* that Lawrence's central affirmations are made most convincingly. These two novels were started as one, but became two when Lawrence found the issues being dealt with were too complex to be illustrated in the one book, but *Women in Love* is a major and independent novel in its own right, and not simply a continuation of *The Rainbow*.

Both novels have marriage as their main theme, and it should be remembered in relation to what has already been discussed in Chapter 2 that Lawrence's insistence on the importance of sexual relationships is in no sense pornographic or sordid. Marriage is the central concern of both of these novels (although in *Women in Love* the importance of other, non-sexual relationships is also emphasised), and marriage is the essential means through which man can come into direct contact with nature and hence, in Lawrence's eyes, achieve moral awareness. A comparison here with Tolstoy, a novelist with whom Lawrence has much in common, will make the point of the exact importance which Lawrence places upon sex and marriage. In Tolstoy's early work before his conversion, particularly in *War and Peace*, marriage retains and nourishes that moral understanding of life which Pierre Bezukhov has already glimpsed from a contact with the external world of nature. Pierre's love for Natasha is suggested by Tolstoy as being essentially a moral force which leads him to live a finer life, although in Tolstoy there is an important corollary to this in his insistence that the real significance of marriage lies in whole family relationships and not only in the awareness, moral and other, that husband and wife may derive from each other. In Lawrence, however, the actual physical sexual relationship provides the final and real moral contact. The external, other-than-human world of nature around us is recognised and emphasised by Lawrence, and the sense of it pervades the early novels, particularly *The White Peacock* and *Sons and Lovers*, but nowhere is it suggested that this external world can in itself properly inform the moral understanding (only in a later novel, *Kangaroo*, is this suggested, and then only tentatively). In *Sons and Lovers*, as we have seen, Paul Morel fails in his personal relationships and this nearly destroys him: nature in itself cannot save him although it helps in strengthening his resolve at the close of the book.

To Lawrence man becomes part of nature only through sex, and real morality is possible only through sex. It may well be thought that Lawrence's own definitions of morality are incomplete and ultimately unconvincing, although this is not to assert that his ideas on human conduct are not important. The themes of his novels—especially *The Rainbow* and *Women in Love*—are 'moral' ones inasmuch as they deal with the problem of personal conduct and the achieving of 'fulfilment' in life. The term 'fulfilment', however, which is Lawrence's own, gives one clue to the limitations of his 'moral' interests, for morality is always explored by Lawrence in predominantly psychological rather than ethical terms, and the relating of an emphasis on sex with the use of the term 'fulfilment' is suggestive of Freud and psycho-analysis. That Lawrence's view of morality was incomplete can be suggested as one major cause of his failure to develop his ideas after the writing of *The Rainbow* and *Women in Love*, and of the uncertainty which enters these novels at various points. The possible limitations in Lawrence's ideas, however, are only incidental to the general excellence of these novels as literature; novels are not moral dissertations.

Readers who come to *The Rainbow* after having read *Sons and Lovers* will notice immediately the marked change in its style and approach, for although like *Sons and Lovers* it could be loosely described as a family chronicle, its technique is far in advance of the earlier book. Whereas *Sons and Lovers* had been written largely in the conventional, 19th-century novelist's tradition of plot and character, *The Rainbow* is markedly a novel of the 20th century in its presentation. Lawrence himself prepares the reader for this in his famous letter to Edward Garnett of 5 June 1914:

> You mustn't look in my novel for the old stable *ego* of the character. There is another *ego*, according to whose action the individual is unrecognisable, and passes through, as it were, allotropic states which it needs a deeper sense than any we've been used to exercise, to discover are states of the same single radically unchanged element. You must not say my novel is shaky—it is not perfect, because I am not expert in what I want to do. But it is the real thing, say what you like. And I shall get my reception, if not now, then before long. Again I say, don't look for the development of the novel to follow the lines of certain characters: the characters fall into the form of some other rhythmic form, as when one draws a fiddle-bow across a fine tray delicately sanded, the sand takes lines unknown.

This is to make clear then that in *The Rainbow* Lawrence is not presenting and delineating his characters in the traditional sense, but is analysing their actions on a deeper psychological level than he had done in his previous novels.

The Rainbow explores the possibilities of the marriage relationship in involved and intricate terms which do not, however, detract from the book's amazing artistic achievement. In the novel Lawrence is concerned with the problem of personal conduct and meaning in life, which he investigates through three generations of the Brangwen family; and in determining exactly what he is saying we must be on our guard against expecting to find any ready-made absolutes or standards which we can pin down. All his characters are concerned with 'the effort of serious living', but the problem which this effort poses is different for each individual and becomes more complicated as the cultural conditions become more sophisticated with each succeeding generation. The first and simplest relationship, in fact, is the only one in which the individuals achieve any sort of fulfilment, although the third part of the novel containing the story of Ursula Brangwen is continued and brought to a fruition in *Women in Love*. In the first generation Tom Brangwen lives a relatively simple life in a 19th-century rural tradition; in the second Will and Anna are faced with the problems of change as the basic rural pattern of their lives is altered; in the third Ursula is faced with all the stresses of modern urban existence.

First Generation: Tom and Lydia

The basic idea behind *The Rainbow* is detailed in the first few pages of the novel. Lawrence has for so long been regarded in the popular mind as praising the flesh at the expense of the spirit that it is perhaps vain to try to absolve him from the charge, but the point of this novel is exactly a reconciliation of the two, body and soul, into a civilised unity. The book begins with a description of the world of the Brangwen men, living in constant contact with nature:

> They felt the rush of the sap in spring, they knew the wave which cannot halt, but every year throws forward the seed to begetting, and falling back, leaves the young-born on the earth. They knew the intercourse between heaven and earth, sunshine drawn into the breast and bowels, the rain sucked up in the daytime, nakedness that comes under the wind in autumn, showing the birds' nests no longer worth hiding. Their life and interrelations were such; feeling the pulse and body of the soil, that opened to their furrow for the grain, and became smooth and supple after their ploughing, and clung to their feet with a weight that pulled like desire, lying hard and unresponsive when the crops were to be shorn away. The young corn waved and was silken, and the lustre slid along the limbs of the men who saw it. p. 2

Yet this world of primitive nature, for all its overpowering beauty, is not enough. The women realise this, and the novel plots a course away from this world but also trying to contain it. Whereas the man is satisfied and contained in nature, to the woman,

> Looking out, as she must, from the front of her house towards the activity of man in the world at large, whilst her husband looked out to the back at sky and harvest and beast and land, she strained her eyes to see what man had done in fighting outwards to knowledge, she strained to hear how he uttered himself in his conquest, her deepest desire hung on the battle that she heard far off, being waged on the edge of the unknown. She also wanted to know, and to be of the fighting host. p. 3

The woman, then, provides in a symbolic sense a keener, sophisticated, civilising influence, which is regarded by Lawrence as 'the anchor and security' of the men. Tom Brangwen, for example, possesses an innate desire 'to find in a woman the embodiment of all his inarticulate, powerful religious impulses' (p. 14) and he does find this in his marriage with Lydia. Marriage gives new meaning to him, making him more deeply a part of nature yet enlarging his experience of life, so that

> Things became so remote and of so little significance, as he knew the powerful source of his life, his eyes opened on a new universe, and he wondered in thinking of his triviality before. p. 54

In fact, when he reviews his life some years later he finds that what it amounts to is his relationship with his wife, through which he has found some sense of fulfilment and meaning. It is marriage which makes him aware of his proper place in nature, and throughout this section of the novel one is aware of the huge backdrop of nature which is brought out so vividly in many scenes, particularly when Tom sets off to propose to Lydia on a March evening with the wind roaring around him. In this context it is useful to remember Lawrence's own perceptive comment on Hardy's *Return of the Native*, a novel which Lawrence is obviously adapting for his own purpose in *The Rainbow*:

> The Heath heaved with raw instinct. Egdon, whose dark soil was strong and crude and organic as the body of a beast. Out of the body

of this crude earth are born Eustacia, Wildeve, Mistress Yeobright, Clym, and all the others. They are one year's accidental crop. What matters if some are drowned or dead, and others preaching or married: what matters, any more than the withering heath, the reddening berries, the seedy furze, and the dead fern of one autumn of Egdon? The Heath persists. Its body is strong and fecund, it will bear many more crops beside this. Here is the sombre latent power that will go on producing, no matter what happens to the product. Here is the deep black source from whence all these little contents of lives are drawn. And the contents of the small lives are spilled and wasted. There is savage satisfaction in it: for so much more remains to come, such a black, powerful fecundity is working there that what does it matter?   PHOENIX, p. 415

Hardy's relationship with Lawrence has never been properly acknowledged by some critics in the past, but it is a profound one. *The Rainbow* may well be conceived in a moral tradition which includes George Eliot on one side as Dr. Leavis has so convincingly argued in *D. H. Lawrence: Novelist*, but it also includes Hardy on another although it may well develop some of Hardy's features almost out of recognition.

The Rainbow is impregnated with this sense of nature conceived in Hardy's sense as not being centred on man but containing its greater meaning in itself, and Tom Brangwen's partial fulfilment and growing sense of moral awareness in this first section of the book are related explicitly to his awareness of this greater process of nature and his part in it. This conception of the relationship of morality and nature implies a sense of *submission*, a word which Lawrence uses often in describing Tom's relationship with Lydia. After she comes to the Brangwen farmhouse to ask for butter, for example, Tom is made aware in her presence of a new awareness which alters him and suspends his own being:

> Since she had come to the house he went about in a daze, scarcely seeing even the things he handled, drifting, quiescent, in a state of metamorphosis. He submitted to that which was happening to him, letting go his will, suffering the loss of himself, dormant always on the brink of ecstasy, like a creature evolving to a new birth.
>
> PP. 33–4

This experience is the basis of Lawrence's whole view of moral awareness. It is an awareness which implies submission of one's own individual will and striving once one has been caught up in the spontaneous process of nature. One might note here that Lawrence presents the relationship between Tom and Lydia with sensitivity and with a marked degree of originality, for there is no suggestion of the values of the romantic love novel in the depiction. That there is true feeling between them cannot be denied, but this 'feeling' is not analysed in the usual clichés of love relationships, and indeed the term 'love' hardly plays any part in the analysis. The nature of their relationship is subtly shown by Lawrence, and their individual wills are caught up and balanced the one against the other.

Second Generation: Will and Anna

The real achievement of Tom Brangwen's life, then, is his ability to submit his will to the wider implication of life, and it is exactly an inability to achieve this which causes the failure in the second generation between Will and Anna. Tom and Lydia achieve a balanced relationship which 'liberates' them, enabling them to 'live from their own centres' whilst dependent the one upon the other. On the other hand, Will (the name is not accidental, and is indeed almost over-obvious) centres himself on Anna and attempts to force her to accept him on his own terms so that neither of them is changed significantly by the other and the marriage is not a new birth of life. From the first and throughout the story the words 'fear', 'shame', 'dread', 'disgrace' are used to comment on Will's attitude, for he refuses to release himself in the way that Tom had done:

> He felt he could not alter from what he was fixed upon, his will was set. To alter it he must be destroyed. And he would not be destroyed.   p. 122

The corn-gathering scene before their marriage symbolises what is to come, and determines the full extent of Will's dependence on Anna. Under 'a large gold moon' the two carry the sheaves of corn in a scene of delicate beauty which is at the same time suggestive of more significance than it at first might appear to possess. The moon-symbol occurs throughout *The Rainbow* and *Women in Love* as an indication of the presence of the sensual, spontaneous world of nature; sometimes the moon is small and distant, suggesting the gulf between this world and the characters, whilst at other times, as here, the moon is huge and pervades the scene. Their love is close to fruition, but the stacking of the sheaves both binds and separates them at once. Anna is always first and 'walked between the moon and his shadowy figure' as a bridge between the world of nature and Will's own self-absorbed being, but he is unable to detach himself from the routine laid down to reach her, and she in her turn makes no effort to help him:

> She saw the moonlight question on his face. But there was a space between them, and he went away, the work carried them, rhythmic. Why was there always a space between them, why were they apart? Why, as she came up from under the moon, would she halt and stand off from him? Why was he held away from her? His will drummed persistently, darkly, it drowned everything else.

> pp. 118–19

In everything he does Will is only interested in confirming the existing way of things. He is afraid of the unknown and seeks comfort and security in Anna, in his work, and in his love of the Church, and all of these are used as chances to escape from rather than to come into contact with life. Anna, for her part, comes to hate Will for his dependence on her and she becomes complete and detached in herself and in her children. At times things go well, but there is no certainty in them, and although Will, like Tom, has to humble himself and admit that without his wife he is nothing, he does this unnaturally through fear and not through a real spontaneous feeling for life as Tom did. Eventually the conflict between Will and Anna ends in defeat for Will, though at the same time hardly in victory for Anna, and the experience at Lincoln Cathedral in Chapter VII (after the one ironically entitled 'Anna Victrix' by Lawrence) details the exact measure of his inevitable defeat. The Church is to

Will the symbol of everything which he holds valuable in life, but Anna (and here she is representing Lawrence's own view of Christianity) sees that for all its real and acknowledged beauty

> it was the ultimate confine. . . . The altar was barren, its lights gone out. God burned no more in that bush. It was dead matter lying there. She claimed the right to freedom above her, higher than the roof. p. 200

In this episode Anna forces Will to realise that there is so much outside his comprehension, that there is something undeveloped in him that will never unfold, and in so doing she destroys his being and entails her own failure to achieve any meaningful existence of her own. She becomes absorbed in her children and loses all interest in life outside them, and the failure in her marriage leads to a failure in the whole life of the family. Children represent an escape from bothering about the immediate issues of life for Anna and Will, and they become immersed in a world of sensual pleasure. Sex to them is not an insight into nature but a reaction against it, for he becomes

> the sensual male seeking his pleasure, she was the female ready to take hers: but in her own way . . . they abandoned in one motion the moral position, each was seeking gratification pure and simple.
> p. 232

This sort of sexual relationship is, and always was, immoral to Lawrence in that it denies the essential experience of life although he was unable to be precise about it in this novel. Its purely animal nature, however, affects the family and Ursula, their eldest daughter, in particular, causing her to look for other values as she grows up:

> The house was a storm of movement. The children were healthy and turbulent, the mother only wanted their animal well-being. To Ursula, as she grew a little older, it became a nightmare. . . . And as a child, she was against her mother, she craved for some spirituality and stateliness. pp. 262–3

Third Generation: Ursula

Growing up in this atmosphere Ursula has from the first a dislike of her mother's self-sufficiency, and she looks out from the home to the outside world to supply some added meaning to life. Her whole development is much more complicated than her parents' or grandparents' had been, and indeed it is so complex that Lawrence was unable to work it out adequately in the one novel and had to break the book into two before being able to deal with it. Even then, as we shall see, it is questionable whether he finally succeeded. The point is that Tom Brangwen's development had begun from the world of nature in his work on the farm, and had been centred on the traditional values of the farmhouse where his family had lived for generations, whilst Ursula has to reject a background that is, at times, a 'nightmare' to her. She must look to the outside world and consequently to a more sophisticated social setting as the scene for her development, and in order to achieve any proper fulfilment must be able to make a finer balance between nature and civilisation than Tom Brangwen had ever needed to do. The question can tentatively be dealt with in terms of class and tradition, in that Ursula is tending towards a more middle-class attitude in becoming more sophisticated. Her parents had disturbed the Brangwen tradition of living off the land, and an element of detachment from nature is evident in their lives. Lawrence's views on class at this time are quite explicit; *Sons and Lovers* had emphasised his respect for traditional working-class values and his suspicion of middle-class ones. In *The Rainbow* this distinction is investigated and confirmed in Ursula's relationship with Skrebensky, and a hint of what is to come is found quite early on when they meet the bargeman, where Ursula

> went hastening on, gladdened by having met the grimy, lean man with the ragged moustache. He gave her a pleasant warm feeling. He made her feel the richness of her own life. Skrebensky, somehow, had created a deadness round her, a sterility, as if the world were ashes. p. 314

The relationship with Skrebensky fails for much the same reasons as the marriage between Ursula's parents had failed. Like Will, Skrebensky is afraid to grasp what is offered him, as it represents so much that is different from the social world of which he is so completely a part. The difference between Will and Skrebensky lies in the fact that the latter is more chained by his pre-conditioned social attitudes, so that if his particular failure is more excusable its social implications are much more important. Skrebensky insists on uncritically accepting the social conceptions of love, duty, patriotism, and the like. Ursula's rejection of him is also a rejection of the social world which he represents and a damning criticism of it, but it almost entails her failure in the same way that her mother had failed, and it is only her intuitive awareness of this which allows her to escape through her realisation that

> to limit, as her mother did, everything to the ring of physical considerations, and complacently to reject the reality of anything else, was horrible. p. 352

The parallel between the two relationships is intended to illustrate all the more clearly Ursula's particular development beyond her mother's view of life, for Ursula defeats Skrebensky as Anna had defeated Will. Ursula makes Skrebensky realise the utter meaninglessness of the social activity which he has prized so much:

> He too realised what England would be in a few hours' time—a blind, sordid, strenuous activity—all for nothing, fuming with dirty smoke and running trains and groping in the bowels of the earth, all for nothing. p. 465

Yet he is too much a part of it to be able to extricate himself and still attempts to force Ursula into it on his terms. The problem of how Ursula was to escape it was complex, and there is a growing sense of uncertainty in the novel as to how her fulfilment would be obtained.

Ursula has spurned one aspect of mere physical nature in her mother and one aspect of society in Skrebensky; she can be said to have rejected false nature and false civilisation. There is, however, an inexactness in defining her own values. She realises, for example, that knowledge of the right sort is important, and refuses to marry Anthony Schofield because he is unable to give

65

her anything more than physical satisfaction and security. Knowledge is vital, yet she insists on retaining a proportionate sense of its value, realising that it is inadequate by itself unless it informs a live relationship between man and the universe beyond him. Thus she rejects her life at the University, for example, as we have mentioned in Chapter I. Lawrence's central affirmation is made more forcibly towards the end of the book, where Ursula is approaching the degree of self-realisation which is to be properly exploited in *Women in Love*. Ursula sees that

> this world in which she lived was a circle lighted by a lamp. This lighted area, lit up by man's completest consciousness, she thought was all the world; that here all was disclosed for ever. Yet all the time, within the darkness she had been aware of points of light, like the eyes of wild beasts, gleaming, penetrating, vanishing. And her soul had acknowledged in a great heave of terror only the outer darkness . . .   p. 437

Ursula realises this in general terms, but the conception is wide and consequently vague. Skrebensky has failed to open this world out to her, and in spite of her real development she is still only half-formed—'that which she was, positively, was dark and unrevealed, it could not come forth'. The extent of her problem is illustrated by Lawrence in the last chapter of the novel, but no satisfactory conclusion is given to it. Having lost her way in the country she is caught amongst a group of horses driven wild by the weather, and she vacillates between a fear of the power of nature symbolised by them and a hesitation about returning to the social world. Even when she escapes the terrible horses she is still indecisive:

> The way was open before her, to the gate in the high hedge in the near distance, so she could pass into the smaller, cultivated field, and so out to the high-road and the ordered world of man. Her way was clear. She lulled her heart. Yet her heart was couched with fear, couched with fear all along.   p. 488

Her dilemma is real and terrible, and Lawrence cannot resolve it. The novel ends on an unreal note of optimism with the symbol of the rainbow which Ursula sees from her sick-room, but she has been forced into this temporary feeling of consolation without sound justification. We realise that Ursula is getting somewhere in her life and sympathise with her that 'she grasped and groped to find the creation of the living God, instead of the old, hard barren form of bygone living', but where exactly has she reached? Lawrence was aware of the difficulty he had in illustrating Ursula's development in acceptable terms, and broke the novel off here to detail her predicament more exactly in *Women in Love*.

'WOMEN IN LOVE'

Women in Love opens with a discussion between Ursula and Gudrun Brangwen about marriage, and the novel goes on to explore the contrasted relationships each sister experiences, maintaining the success of one and failure of the other to find any real fulfilment. Lawrence's intention in writing the book was to deal more exactly with the themes of *The Rainbow* in a contemporary setting, and to work out an acceptable solution to Ursula's problems as they had been presented in the earlier novel. Marriage was to be the key to meaningful existence and the solution to the ills of mechanical civilisation, with the perfect Lawrentian relationship presented through Ursula's and Birkin's achievement. In fact, the affirmations Lawrence intended to make become increasingly questionable as the novel progresses, and although it makes several important assertions its overall impact is weakened by Lawrence's growing suspicion that it was not possible completely to found a whole way of life on the marriage relationship. It is worth noting, for example, that *Women in Love*, like *The Rainbow*, ends on a note of indecision with Birkin unsure of the total value of marriage. Lawrence, it should be added, does not question the basic worth of marriage, but becomes doubtful as to whether it is ultimately sufficient, as Birkin had realised in an earlier conversation with Gerald:

I do believe in a permanent union between a man and a woman. Chopping about is merely an exhaustive process. But a permanent relation between a man and a woman isn't the last word—it certainly isn't. pp. 344–5

Birkin

It is wrong to regard the two contrasted relationships between Ursula and Birkin and between Gerald and Gudrun simply and unequivocally in terms of a contrast between the good and the bad. Gerald may fail in his life for what are perhaps valid reasons, but it is utterly wrong to regard Birkin, for his part, as a clear thread of light running through the novel. Birkin is often confused and contradictory, especially in the early part of the novel, and although he does progress during the course of it so many of its bad features are connected with him that the artistic weakness evident in his portrayal indicates a profound uncertainty in Lawrence himself as to Birkin's genuineness. This uncertainty of tone is the most distinguishing feature of *Women in Love* when compared to *The Rainbow*, and is evident from both Birkin's activities—such as the wrestling-scene and his wish for a *blutbruderschaft* with Gerald, and the scene in which he lies naked amidst the daisies in Chapter VIII—and also from Lawrence's style. At times the quality of the writing in *Women in Love* falls away sharply, and Lawrence's own uncertainty shows itself in the jargon and over-emphasis of several passages too unpleasant to quote. Birkin's positive beliefs are often vague and confused. He refuses to accept love as an absolute with Ursula, but he is unsure what to put in its place:

> 'And if you don't believe in love, what *do* you believe in?' she asked mocking. 'Simply in the end of the world, and grass?'
> He was beginning to feel a fool.
> 'I believe in the unseen hosts,' he said. p. 121

Yet he has already insisted earlier on in conversation with Gerald (in the chapter 'In the Train') that love for a woman must be the centre of a man's life, and is almost angry with Gerald for being cynical about such an idea. Birkin's confusion mirrors Lawrence's own, and although such indecision may be typical of real life it causes a dramatic failure in terms of literature in the working out of the ideas in the novel. Birkin does develop his ideas and comes to accept the value of marriage in spite of his early waverings, but never as forcefully or convincingly as Tom Brangwen had been able to accept it in *The Rainbow*. In the chapter 'Moony', for example, Birkin is discovered by Ursula stoning the moon's image in Willey Water:

> 'Cybele—curse her! The accursed Syria Dea! Does one begrudge it her? What else is there—?'
>
> Ursula wanted to laugh loudly and hysterically, hearing his isolated voice speaking out. It was so ridiculous.
>
> He stood staring at the water. Then he stooped and picked up a stone, which he threw sharply at the pond. Ursula was aware of the bright moon leaping and swaying, all distorted, in her eyes.
>
> pp. 238–9

Lawrence's mythology may be a little confused, but Syria Dea and Cybele can be loosely said to represent female superiority in some form, and calling the moon by these names brings right out into the open the underlying meaning of the moon symbol used throughout *The Rainbow* and *Women in Love* in almost every important scene. Here the moon explicitly represents the vital sensual aspect of nature and marriage, which Birkin at this moment would like to be able to repudiate. In trying to shatter the moon's image Birkin is attempting to deny his need for Ursula, who in her turn identifies herself with the moon:

> Ursula was dazed, her mind was all gone. She felt she had fallen to the ground and was spilled out, like water on the earth.   p. 240

The symbolism is so delicate that discussing its meaning so openly can easily harm it, and I have deliberately refrained from mining out all its obvious significance. Birkin, of course, cannot shatter the moon's image. It rebuilds itself on the rippled water, and he realises that his need for Ursula cannot be denied. The proposal to her, in fact, comes soon after this scene in the same chapter. Yet again there is still some doubt in Birkin's (and in Lawrence's) mind.

Birkin sees that his only salvation is through marriage with Ursula, yet the temporary rebuff he experiences from her when he proposes makes him question such an idea. In the chapter 'Gladiatorial' which immediately follows 'Moony', Birkin tries to establish an additional relationship with Gerald, suspecting that even if he does marry Ursula marriage will not be ultimately sufficient. The bathos of this scene harks back to Birkin's earlier wish for a *blutbruderschaft* with Gerald, and again emphasises the uncertainty underlying the book. It would be wrong to exaggerate this uncertainty, which after all only weakens but does not cripple the novel, but it is present in everything Birkin does and must make suspect his relationship with Ursula. Lawrence, through Birkin, begins to be unsure about everything, even sex:

> 'Fusion, fusion, this horrible fusion of two beings, which every woman and most men insisted on, was it not nauseous and horrible anyhow, whether it was a fusion of the spirit or of the emotional body? . . . Ursula was the perfect Womb, the bath of birth, to which all men must come. . . . Why not leave the other being free, why try to absorb, or melt, or merge?'   p. 301

This nausea does not last, of course, and almost immediately after this in the same chapter, entitled 'Excurse', Birkin and Ursula come to realise Lawrence's view of the true meaning of sex, although here again the description has none of the lyrical assurance of *The Rainbow* or even of *Lady Chatterley's Lover*. Moreover, now that the marriage is agreed upon, Birkin's one wish is to travel, anywhere and as soon as possible, which seems quite justifiably suspicious to Ursula:

> Wandering seemed to her like restlessness, dissatisfaction.
> 'Where will you wander to?' she asked.
> 'I don't know. I feel as if I would just meet you and we'd set off— just towards the distance. . . . That's the thing to do—let's wander off.'
> 'Yes—' she said, thrilled at the thought of travel. But to her it was only travel.
> 'To be free,' he said. 'To be free, in a free place, with a few other people!'
> 'Yes,' she said wistfully. Those 'few other people' depressed her.
>   pp. 307–8

Marriage in Birkin's eyes is not to be a supreme or exclusive relationship; this is expressed in such terms as to cause Ursula much uneasiness. Although Birkin is the central character of *Women in Love* (the shift of emphasis from Ursula being a radical change from the plan suggested in *The Rainbow*) it still remains true that Ursula has most commonsense about the ideas discussed in it, almost as if Birkin represented Lawrence's desire to find a wholly satisfactory relationship and Ursula his knowledge that nothing so ultimately satisfying was to be found. In spite of all qualifications, however, marriage is meant to be Birkin's salvation, and although the novel fails to convince the reader that such salvation is right and inevitable, marriage does offer the only convincing basis for Birkin's life when set against the other possibilities as Lawrence presents them.

Birkin has to face two temptations during the course of the novel which attempt to give order to his life outside his relationship with Ursula. Before he meets her he sees that life appears to give him a choice between two evils—that he can either accept Gerald's way of dealing with life, the mechanical social aspect of contemporary civilisation, or else react violently against this in a purely sensual, extremely 'natural' way, as symbolised by the African carving he sees in Halliday's flat. The carving, in fact, is by far the greater temptation, and Birkin is enthusiastic about it the first time it is mentioned, seeing in it

> Pure culture in sensation, culture in the physical consciousness, really ultimate *physical* consciousness, mindless, utterly sensual. It is so sensual as to be final, supreme. p. 72

The carving represents a 'return to nature' in its worst and most extreme sense, which appeals to Birkin in that, superficially at least, it seems the exact opposite of his contemporary, over-civilised, purely rational and mechanical world. Too much intellect is bad, therefore revert to pure sensuality for a while in order to regain a proper balance. In fact, this argument, as Birkin realises, is too glib and simple. In the chapter 'Moony', after the scene at Willey Water, Birkin becomes aware of Ursula as an escape from having to choose between the devil of sensuality and the deep blue sea of the social world. The solution he reaches is important. The carving symbolises a sensuality which he must reject:

> Suddenly he found himself face to face with a situation. It was as simple as this: fatally simple. On the one hand he knew he did not want a further sensual experience—something deeper, darker, than ordinary life could give. He remembered the African fetishes he had seen at Halliday's so often. There came back to him one, a statuette from West Africa, in dark wood, glossy and suave. It was a woman, with hair dressed high, like a melon-shaped dome.... She knew what he himself did not know. She had thousands of years of purely sensual, purely unspiritual knowledge behind her. It must have been thousands of years since her race had died, mystically: that is, since the relation between the senses and the outspoken mind had broken, leaving the experience all in one sort, mystically sensual. Thousands of years ago, that which was imminent in himself must have taken place in these Africans: the goodness, the holiness, the desire for creation and productive happiness must have lapsed, leaving the single impulse for knowledge in one sort, mindless progressive knowledge through the senses, knowledge arrested and ending in the senses, mystic knowledge in disintegration and dissolution, knowledge such as the beetles have, which live purely within the world of corruption and cold dissolution.... Was this then all that remained? ... There was another way, the way of freedom. There was the paradisal entry into pure, single being, the individual soul taking precedence over love and desire for union, stronger than any pangs of emotion, a lovely state of free proud singleness, which accepted the obligation of the permanent connection with others, and with the other, submits to the yoke and leash of love, but never forfeits its own proud individual singleness, even while it loves and yields.   p. 245–7

Birkin knows that he must reject this sensual world as it implies dissolution and corruption. His imaginative and intelligent insight, in fact, puts paid to Rousseau's 'Noble Savage' myth once and for all by carrying it to its logical conclusion in grasping the essential dissolute quality of the savages. It is impossible to revert to their world, as Lawrence realised in his discussion of

72

Melville's *Typee* and *Omoo* in the brilliant *Studies in Classic American Literature*:

> We can't go back. We can't go back to the savages: not a stride. We can take a great curve in their direction onwards. But we cannot turn the current of our life backwards, back towards their soft warm twilight and uncreate mud. Not for a moment. If we do it for a moment, it makes us sick.   p. 130

The purely primitive is never enough in Lawrence's writing. Just as the woman who rode away rode to her death, Lawrence rejects the primitive in this novel even more forcefully than he had done in *The Rainbow*. One cannot revert in this way, but at the same time one cannot accept the contemporary solution as Gerald does. The African way and the contemporary way are, in fact, similar through their very opposition. The Africans had denied the intellect in the same way as 20th-century man was denying the senses, and just as the result for the Africans was dissolute sensuality so Gerald and Gudrun too are dissolute and depraved inwardly:

> The vindictive mockery in her voice made his brain quiver. Glancing up at him, into his eyes, she revealed again the mocking, white-cruel recognition. There was league between them, abhorrent to them both. They were implicated with each other in abhorrent mysteries.   p. 234

Gerald and Gudrun

Lawrence's insight into the characters of Gerald and Gudrun is often more convincing and moving than Birkin's consummation with Ursula, and indeed the real force of the book does seem to lie in the analysis of Gerald and Gudrun, that is, more in its negative than in its positive aspects. In the novel Lawrence is a prophet crying in the wilderness of a mechanical civilisation that threatens to destroy itself, and through an investigation of the relationship between Gerald and Gudrun he illustrates the potential dangers of mechanised society with its mechanically thinking individuals. Gerald Crich represents the self-destructive and meaningless effort of modern industrial society:

> 'Certainly, he's got go,' said Gudrun. 'In fact I've never seen a man that showed signs of so much. The unfortunate thing is, where does his *go* go to, what becomes of it?' p. 41

As we see, nothing becomes of it. Gerald fails to find meaning or fulfilment in life and is destroyed, and his failure is seen to arise directly out of his inability to accept his proper place in nature. His attitude to nature is seen in many places, most important perhaps in the chapter 'Coal Dust' where he forces the horse to remain at the level crossing in spite of its terror at the passing train. His desire to master and dominate the horse is really a desire to dominate nature, a feature which is further brought out in the chapter 'Rabbit', and which binds him to Gudrun. She too has an inherent hatred of instinctive life and a desire to pacify it, as Ursula realises in the episode with the robins in 'Moony' (pp. 256–7). The important chapter 'Rabbit' confirms Gerald and Gudrun in an unholy alliance, and love to them is a matter of mere sensuality. Gerald, however, as we already know, has denied in conversation with Birkin that love could really be the centre of his own life and has doubted many of Birkin's positive views about marriage (Chapter V, 'In the Train'). Marriage can offer little to Gerald, in fact, because the relationship is so uneven. Gudrun dominates him from the start, although Lawrence fails to make the reasons explicit:

> The bond was established between them, in that look, in her tone. In her tone, she made the understanding clear—they were of the same kind, he and she, a sort of diabolic freemasonary subsisted between them. Henceforward, she knew, she had her power over him. Wherever they met, they would be secretly associated. And he would be helpless in the association with her. Her soul exulted.
>
> p. 114

There is no question of any kind of balance in this relationship, in the sense that the term was used in the discussion of *The Rainbow*. It is an alliance of sensuality and pleasure, for both Gerald and Gudrun are worried only by the pleasure-principle in discussing their possible marriage, so that in his heart of hearts Gerald knows that it really offers him little hope:

74

Marriage was like a doom to him. He was willing to condemn himself in marriage, to become like a convict condemned to the mines of the underworld, living no life in the sun, but having a dreadful subterranean activity. He was willing to accept this. p. 345

Gerald denies the natural order of life in his denial of real marriage, and this denial is a part of his wilful desire to control rather than submit to nature. He fails to realise the power of nature, by the side of which his own power is negligible and meaningless. Gudrun and he 'felt powerful enough to leap over the confines of life into the forbidden places, and back again' (p. 389). It is this conceit which kills him.

Lawrence's Moral Sense

Gerald's failure is a failure to establish any connection between himself and the reality of nature, and consequently, as one would expect, an inability to achieve any kind of fulfilment. The question is, of course, whether his failure is consequently immoral or merely amoral—that is, how far morality really enters into the discussion at all. Lawrence himself hardly uses the term 'moral' or its opposite in either *The Rainbow* or *Women in Love*, whilst his critics appear to be unable to use any other word. On what terms is Lawrence criticising Gerald and praising Birkin? Gerald is obviously regarded as being wrong in his attitude to nature, but how could he have been different? Can Birkin, with his bathetic offer of a *blutbruderschaft*, seriously be considered as offering Gerald a valid means of altering his whole being? The question can be made larger in asking how Gerald or Skrebensky or Will Brangwen could change their whole beings and achieve fulfilment. How could Will lose his fear, or Skrebensky or Gerald their reliance on the social system? The unfortunate conclusion is that no answer can be understood from Lawrence's writings. The fulfilment through marriage is in itself a fulfilment between special kinds of people, between people who are ready for a fulfilment which marriage only develops. Moral responsibility implies a freedom of being which Lawrence takes for granted in Tom Brangwen, Birkin and Ursula, and denies Gerald and Will. Thus Gerald's failure can hardly be described as a *moral* one, as the question of any valid freedom of choice never really arises for him. Lawrence is always placing his finger in the balance and tipping it against Gerald. The reader never *blames* Gerald, but only feels sympathy for him.

This should tend to make suspect Birkin's own achievement. Lawrence's uncertainty in detailing this has already been stressed and there is no need to repeat it here, but the problem of how far Birkin's fulfilment is a moral one has still to be faced. The point I am trying to establish is that Birkin's fulfilment is 'moral' only in the most general use of that word, in that he 'becomes what he is' or 'finds himself' through marriage, and added meaning is given to his life by it only at the expense of much doubt. The extent of this doubt should make us hesitate to call Birkin's attitudes moral—there is no feeling of moral perfection about him nor any recognition in any of the other characters that he is morally superior. Marriage fails to give him an overall and thoroughly convincing insight into the reality of nature, and there is a major discrepancy between the novel's most important affirmation and the tone of Birkin's relationship with Ursula. This affirmation is contained in the last few pages of the book and harks back in feeling to the most compelling pages of *The Rainbow*. It contains an insight which denies man's importance in the universe in favour of something greater:

> Whatever the mystery which has brought forth man and the universe, it is a non-human mystery, it has its own great ends, man is not the criterion. Best leave it all to the vast, creative, non-human mystery. Best strive with oneself only, not with the universe.
>
> 'God cannot do without man.' It was a saying of some great French religious teacher. But surely this is false. God can do without man. God could do without the ichthyosauri and the mastodon. These monsters failed creatively to develop, so God, the creative mystery, dispensed with them. In the same way the mystery could dispense with man, should he too fail creatively to change and develop ...
> pp. 469–70

One feels, however, that this is Lawrence speaking here, not Birkin. Birkin's marriage with Ursula is fraught with too much doubt to come alive on the page with real impassioned life as, say, Tom Brangwen's came alive in *The Rainbow*. This profound insight into life does not seem to arise easily and naturally out of Birkin's marriage, but rather to have been grafted on by Lawrence. One never feels this marriage possesses the significance which one felt Tom Brangwen's marriage to possess—one is merely told it is meaningful and asked to accept it. Because of the strong impression of personal integrity which comes through in both novels one is forced to consider seriously Lawrence's statements, but final conviction does not always strike home in *Women in Love*.

SUMMING-UP

It must be stressed again that in criticising *Women in Love* the intention is not to give the impression that Lawrence's basic insistence on marriage and his regard for nature is wholly misguided and misconceived. The amazing artistic achievement of *The Rainbow* confirms the importance of Lawrence's ideas at a profound and entirely meaningful level. What has been done is to suggest that Lawrence himself had become aware during the course of writing these two novels that the marriage relationship was not enough upon which to build one's whole life. It is important but not wholly and ultimately sufficient. It gives a sense of purpose and fulfilment to life to a certain, inevitably limited extent, and Lawrence merely became increasingly aware of these limitations in *Women in Love*. Lawrence was unable to define this sense of fulfilment in really valid terms and the extent to which this 'fulfilment' is wholly a moral one is open to some doubt.

That the 'fulfilment' Lawrence speaks of is not so easily equated with 'moral awareness', except in the most general sense of the term (as many of Lawrence's present critics tend to assume), is evidenced by the novels which follow *Women in Love*. In these later novels Lawrence tries to establish the proper course of action for the fulfilled individual outside the marriage relation-ship in the social world of men. The fact that this fulfilment achieved in *The Rainbow* and *Women in Love* is not essentially and explicitly moral leads to a failure in Lawrence to develop his ideas beyond the point reached by Birkin, as we shall see. These two novels had dealt with society in so far as it touched on the theme of marriage and the individual, but now the outlook was to become wider. Marriage, we have learnt from the experience of Birkin, does not appear to be enough. Nature must learn something from society and teach something to society. The theme of the two novels so far discussed had been a reconciliation of nature and civilisation, involving a proper understanding of both. On a general level Lawrence's intention was to restate the need of bringing together these two worlds of man and nature, of pastoral simplicity and civilised sophistication, which has been a perennial theme in literature. The idea is similar in outline to that of Shakespeare's last plays or the medieval romance of *Sir Gawain and the Green Knight*, with one important qualification. To Shakespeare and the medieval poet, there is a split between man and nature which is resolved symbolically through the story, with no great difficulty, in moving and compelling yet simple terms; whereas in Lawrence the situation is more complex. The split between society and nature has become immense. Society has become almost a complete evil in itself in that it exists not simply by ignoring nature but by attempting to control and pacify it. In *Cymbeline* the court was ignorant of the country, and Belarius attempted to make Guiderius and Arviragus ignorant of the court, by bringing up his nephews in a natural, pastoral setting far removed from the evils of courtly, 'civilised' behaviour. Shakespeare sets his characters in two main symbolic groups, of courtly sophistication and primitive simplicity, and through the character of Imogen these two groups are brought to a finer understanding of life and a realisation that each needs the virtues of the other. In *Women in Love*, however, Gerald refuses to make any compromise with the world of nature. He attempts to dictate to it, totally refusing to recognise its power or importance. Through his character the social world of industry is shown to have become out of hand, and Lawrence now tries to analyse contemporary man's relationship with society in more exact terms in his succeeding novels.

5

Lawrence's Later Novels

In *The Rainbow* and *Women in Love* Lawrence had concerned himself with the problem of achieving fulfilment in life, and had suggested marriage as the means of obtaining this fulfilment for his characters and for himself. The relationship between Ursula and Birkin in *Women in Love* is at once meant by Lawrence to be the ideal solution to those problems with which he had to deal, and it is also the beginning of a new and larger problem. *Women in Love* ended on a note of indecision as to what in fact Birkin had actually achieved: his marriage to Ursula is shown as possessing some considerable positive value, but there is doubt as to its completeness—a feeling either that complete fulfilment cannot after all be found in marriage, or that Lawrence cannot see where one is to go when one is fulfilled in this way. The problem of conduct remains increasingly pressing. What is the fulfilled man to *do*? How should he spend his time and energies? Should he engage in political activity, and, if so, in what sort of political activity? Or should he spend his time cultivating his own garden, ignoring the condition of the world around him, secure in his own little world of apparent meaning? Lawrence's later novels, which I shall discuss in this chapter—mainly *Aaron's Rod*, *Kangaroo*, and *Lady Chatterley's Lover* (as well as *The Plumed Serpent*, and the long short story *St. Mawr*, which we shall mention only in passing)—take up the problem where it was left in *Women in Love*. Each of these novels deals with the problem in a different way, and none of them comes near a solution more satisfying than that already found in *The Rainbow* and *Women in Love*, nor do they on the whole possess the force or literary appeal of the earlier works. Yet diverse in quality as

79

they are, these later novels are not without interest both as literature and as explorations in search of new values in their attempts to develop the basic ideas in a wider social framework.

These later novels, of course, like much of Lawrence's work, are intimately related to his own life, and the characters in them often bear a striking resemblance to the author himself. In the first chapter some mention has been made of Lawrence's own life and the reader is reminded of the factors which Lawrence felt drove him out of England in 1919, as soon as he could get away after the end of the First World War. Each reader must make his own evaluation of the rationality of Lawrence's arguments about the deplorable level to which civilisation in Britain had sunk during the Great War, and it is not easy to conclude how much of Lawrence's loathing (at times almost mounting to hysteria) of England which is echoed in the later novels is due to an objective assessment of the nature of English society, and how much to a personal feeling of persecution and rejection. Chapter XII of *Kangaroo* (subtitled 'The Nightmare') gives Lawrence's own point of view in a most vivid and dramatic way, and more people today are likely to sympathise with his opinion of the country and the war than did most of those at the time. It is worth noting that only *Lady Chatterley's Lover* of the major later novels is set entirely in England: *Aaron's Rod* (1922) starts in England but soon moves to Italy; *Kangaroo* (1923) and *The Plumed Serpent* (published 1926) are the results of Lawrence's occasionally curious impressions of Australia and Mexico respectively.

'AARON'S ROD'

Aaron's Rod, the earliest novel of this last group, is a patchy work which departs violently from the sexual preoccupations of the earlier novels. Aaron Sisson, its hero, leaves his wife at the beginning of the book, and regrets both the sexual experiences he has during it. Aaron is a miner in a Nottinghamshire village who one day walks out on his wife and goes first to London and then to Italy in pursuit of a more meaningful life (the rod of the title refers to the flute which Aaron plays, but has obvious

Freudian overtones). Lilly, the other main character, is away from his wife for most of the novel and is important not because of his sexual relationship with her but because of his friendship with Aaron. The book itself has a tentative air about it, and Lawrence seems to be writing with no clear idea of where he is going. Aaron and Lilly are made the central figures of the story in the hope, one imagines, of a solution emerging from them by the time the story ends. Lawrence in *Women in Love* had attempted to let Birkin find a purposeful existence beyond marriage in his friendship with Gerald, but there it had failed because of Gerald's own character. Here, in *Aaron's Rod*, Lawrence creates Aaron and Lilly congenial to each other in a way in which Birkin and Gerald never could have been. Lawrence, it would seem, felt convinced that the added meaning he was searching for was to be found between men where there were (on the surface at least) no sexual complications. *Aaron's Rod*, of course, fails to resolve the problem, and it is not difficult to see why. The fulfilment obtained by Birkin and Ursula and preached by Lawrence was basically a physical, sexual concept. Meaning relied on physical communion and feeling, which one would expect normally to be absent from any relationship between men. Moreover, the relationship between Aaron and Lilly is not one between two separate individuals so much as between two aspects of Lawrence's own self—both Aaron and Lilly are Lawrence himself in different guises. Aaron is a realistic character, but Lilly has the air of being just a mouthpiece for Lawrentian doctrines. He is insufficiently realised, and is interesting to the reader only through what he says—not because of what he does or is. Lilly's part in the novel is to play the Good Angel to Aaron's Everyman. The novel itself is meant to represent Aaron reaching a state of fulfilment outside of any sexual relationship, but whether he approaches this state is doubtful, for in his rather picaresque adventures there is little progression of character through the course of the novel. He is as interesting at the beginning of the novel as he is at the end. From the first he has a contempt for the conventional ideals which govern society, and Lilly does little to deepen this attitude.

Yet although everything in *Aaron's Rod* is doubtful and Aaron fails to achieve a more realistic fulfilment than he already possesses, and in spite of the fact that Lilly is undeveloped as a character and is quite the dullest and least pleasant embodiment of Lawrence himself in all his works, the novel is not without merit. It may contain more unadulterated talk than any other of Lawrence's works, yet the talk is often illuminating and sensible. The social criticism is less developed than it was in *Women in Love* or than it is to be in *Lady Chatterley's Lover*, and the only real indication of its presence is to be found in the criticism Aaron makes of Sir William Franks, where the money factor, and that alone, is seen to have raised Franks to the exalted position of respect that he commands. Yet there is also a veiled form of social criticism in Aaron's experiences in cutting right across class divisions, for he is made to realise the existence of the same meaninglessness in all levels of society. In spite of all this, however, *Aaron's Rod* is indecisive, and Lawrence knew it.

'KANGAROO'

Kangaroo investigates and rejects the possibility raised in *Aaron's Rod* of political activity as a meaningful outlet for the fulfilled man's energies. It should be noted at once that in one respect *Kangaroo* is very different from all Lawrence's other major novels in that most of it was written at high speed in the space of about six weeks, and that the first draft is also the final published version. Mention has been made elsewhere of Lawrence's usual custom of working very hard on the writing of a novel: usually the novel is revised completely at least once after the completion of the first draft. As I have suggested before, the notion of D. H. Lawrence as being an unskilled, unsophisticated writer is belied by the care with which most of the major novels except *Kangaroo* are worked on before the final published draft. The speed with which *Kangaroo* was written partly explains (although it does not excuse) the journalistic cliché-ridden quality of some of the writing.

At the same time I would stress the positive virtues which the novel possesses, for although it is not a work of superb literary artistry in the sense that *The Rainbow* at least can be said to be, it has been often underestimated. The plot of the novel concerns the experiences of Richard Lovat Somers in the Australia of the 1920s. Somers is a writer, and is obviously D. H. Lawrence himself in one of his not too effective disguises, although the events of the book are not very close to Lawrence's own experiences. Lawrence was only in Australia for a little over three months (from the end of April to early August 1922), and spent most of his time in the small coastal town of Thirroul in New South Wales, about forty miles south of Sydney, living in a house overlooking the Pacific with the (unhappily) typically Australian name of 'Wyewurk'. In the novel Somers is introduced by an Australian friend, Jack Callcott, to a semi-fascist organisation set up by a group of ex-servicemen in Sydney, which is led in a rather unlikely way by Ben Cooley, the Kangaroo of the novel's title. Somers seems interested at first in becoming involved in this movement and for much of the novel he toys with the idea of joining it, although he also thinks of becoming involved with the socialist movement later on. What Somers is searching for is

> to do something with living people, somewhere, somehow, while I live on the earth. I write, but I write alone. And I live alone. Without any connection whatever with the rest of men.   p. 66

He associates with the Diggers movement led by Ben Cooley, but well before the end of the novel he has not surprisingly rejected both the movement and its leader, and the real appeal of the novel does not actually lie in the 'political' story of Somers's relations with Ben Cooley so much as in the descriptions of the Australian natural scene which Lawrence writes with such force. Yet the two aspects are related, for whilst Kangaroo and Somers are talking and arguing, behind them all the time is this sense of the immensity and the terror of the natural scene. The device is roughly similar to that used by Hardy in *The Return of the Native*, where Egdon Heath dwarfs much of the human effort made in the book, although in *Kangaroo* the device is not so deliberate and does not obtrude itself so skilfully on to the story as it does in Hardy. In *Kangaroo*, civilised life in Australia is there only on the surface:

> There was the vast town of Sydney. And it didn't seem to be real, it seemed to be sprinkled on the surface of a darkness into which it never penetrated.   p. 8

and again in Chapter II:

> There is the wide Pacific rolling in on the yellow sand: the wide fierce sea that makes all the built-over land dwindle into non-existence.   p. 19

There is a sense of human life being lived precariously on the edge of something huge and magnificent, as Somers discovers on his walk into the Bush in the opening chapter. The sea and the Bush are always there to remind one constantly of man's insignificance in the natural order, and they dominate the novel.

With the knowledge of all this around him, Somers has difficulty from the first in really interesting himself in political activity. Initially the main interest of Australia for Lawrence is caught up with the similarity between the Australian situation and Somers's own:

> The absence of any inner meaning: and at the same time the great sense of vacant spaces. The sense of irresponsible freedom. The sense of do-as-you-please liberty. All utterly uninteresting. What is more hopelessly uninteresting than accomplished liberty? Great swarming teeming Sydney flowing out into these myriads of bungalows, like shallow waters spreading, undyked. And what then? Nothing. No inner life, no high command, no interest in anything, finally. . . . Poor Richard Lovat wearied himself to death struggling with the problem of himself, and calling it Australia.
>
>   p. 22

However, the similarity is not pursued by Lawrence in the book as a whole. The real appeal of *Kangaroo* lies in its evocation of the Australian landscapes and in its assessment of the Australian character. In discussing the 'political' theme of the novel it should be noted that Lawrence is embroidering on the historical facts of the Australian situation in the early 1920s by inventing the semi-fascist returned serviceman's organisation led by Kangaroo, yet in doing this he is being curiously prophetic of the way in which certain elements of the returned serviceman's associations were to develop in succeeding years. Lawrence gives a shrewd analysis of some Australian political attitudes and of national characteristics in his portrayal of the members of Kangaroo's organisation, with their grandiose notions of themselves as the self-appointed guardians of the nation. The character of Jack Callcott in particular, with his ideas of conformity and of the immeasurable worth of the returned serviceman to the nation's welfare, is a magnificently realistic description of some facets of their national character to which Australians then or now will not readily admit. (The novel is not popular in Australia.)

Somers is a little cynical of the validity of some of these attitudes from the start, and he is to some extent brought into contact with Kangaroo against his will, although he has an undefined notion that political activity might help him to find added purpose in life. He never really enters the movement, and from the first, when Jack Callcott tells him about the Diggers,

> Somers was silent, very much impressed, though his heart felt heavy. . . . Politics, conspiracy, political power: it was all so alien to him. Somehow, in his soul he had always meant something quite different, when he thought of action along with other men.
>
> p. 91

What he does want is something different from all this, but like Lawrence's previous heroes, Birkin and Lilly, he is vague when it comes to making any positive statement of his own position:

> Then Jack added his question:
> 'Do you really care about anything, Mr. Somers?'
> Richard turned and looked him for a moment in the eyes. And then, knowing the two men were trying to corner him, he said coolly:
> 'Why, yes, I care supremely.'
> 'About what?' Jack's question was soft as a drop of water falling into water, and Richard sat struggling with himself.
> 'That,' he answered, 'you either know or don't know. And if you don't know, it would only be words my trying to tell.'
> There was a silence of check-mate.   p. 60

Somers here and elsewhere in the book is still unable to define his position precisely. Inevitably he rejects Kangaroo and all he stands for, which is to be a sort of comforting father-figure on a political scale so ludicrous that one wonders how Somers ever came to consider it seriously even for a moment. What Somers puts forward finally as a positive assertion in the book is the very fact of his 'aloneness', his individuality and separateness from all unions and causes:

> That was now all he wanted: to get clear. Not to save humanity or to help humanity or to have anything to do with humanity. No— no. Kangaroo had been his last embrace with humanity. Now, all he wanted was to cut himself clear. . . . To be alone from it all. To cut himself finally clear from the last encircling arm of the octopus humanity. To turn to the old dark gods, who had waited so long in the outer dark. p. 271

Somers attempts to define this attitude as essentially a religious one—to 'get his own soul clear' as he says immediately following the passage just quoted. Somers, like Birkin and Lilly, is sick of human imperfectibility, but unlike them he turns to nature more violently as an escape from it. It is doubtful whether many readers of the novel would agree with or completely understand the 'religious' notions developed in the second half of the book, but the overpowering descriptions of the sea and the Bush at least suggest that Somers's attitude is more than the vulgar spleen of the misanthrope. The magnificent vitality of these descriptions of the world of nature around him prevents the reader from asserting too hastily that Somers's reaction to humanity is one of mere neurotic distress. In the latter part of the novel Lawrence attempts through Somers to achieve a religious insight which is not properly developed and the appeal of which is soon to be lost in the smoke rising from the sacrificial altars of *The Plumed Serpent*. Somers's insights into nature are vividly described, but they *do* nothing to him in the way that similar insights in, say, Wordsworth or Tolstoy affect their characters' whole *moral* beings. To Somers the actual moment of insight is of central importance, but it leads to no moral knowledge: that is, it gives him no clearer idea of how to behave and act. To Lawrence himself the supposedly religious

nature of the insight leads him unhappily into the world of
The Plumed Serpent.

A NOTE ON 'THE PLUMED SERPENT'

Kangaroo does not solve any of Lawrence's problems finally. It
shows an advance on *Aaron's Rod* in the attempt to formulate
a 'religious' sense, but this was not developed enough to provide
a realistic basis for living. This 'religious' sense was to play an
important part in Lawrence's next full-length novel—*The
Plumed Serpent*—where the various strands of his earlier work
were brought together with most unhappy results (a long short
story of Lawrence's Mexican period, *St. Mawr*, published in
1925, sets out the typical features of Lawrence's work more
attractively). In *The Plumed Serpent* Lawrence formulates a new
'religious' system in the unlikely surroundings of Mexico: as the
gods did not exist it was necessary to invent them. The problem
of personal relationships is subsidiary in this novel, in which the
central character is a woman and not another version of Lawrence
himself. The woman, Kate Leslie, visits Mexico and is caught up
in a revolutionary religious movement designed to restore the
old gods to the country. In her relationship with Don Ramon
Cipriano, one of the leaders of the movement, she is alternately
fascinated and repelled by the nature of this organisation, but
eventually she experiences some deeper fulfilment.

Critical opinion of the novel in the past has been almost
unanimously hostile, although more recently some commentators have begun to stress its interest both as an illustration of
Lawrence's ideas and also, perhaps incredibly, because of its
suggested literary merits. That the novel is not entirely without
some redeeming features cannot be denied, particularly in its
evocations of the Mexican landscape, but many readers will find
these outweighed by the quality of much of the other writing
and the nature of the revival of pagan religion as Lawrence
investigates it. It is enough for our purposes here to point out
that there seems to be room for some difference of opinion about
a book which is often held to be easily Lawrence's worst, and
to be fair one should quote Keith Sagar's comment: 'Any

critic might be expected to have reservations about this novel, but the wholesale condemnation it has received is indicative, it seems to me, of far deeper failings in the critics than in the book; and failure to meet the basic critical challenge, the challenge to enter wholly, if only temporarily, into the fictional world. Critics have kept the book at arms' length, with an almost hysterical defensiveness, as if it were not art but propaganda' (*The Art of D. H. Lawrence*, p. 159).

'LADY CHATTERLEY'S LOVER'

Lady Chatterley's Lover is without doubt the best known of all Lawrence's books, although its popularity is of course based largely on the wrong reasons. It is, in fact, a novel with an important social theme, although it has a slightly artificial (almost fairy-tale) quality about it which is reminiscent of some of his short stories such as *Daughters of the Vicar*. On the surface it is unrelated to the other novels discussed in this chapter (it was written between 1925–8). It does take up definite positions in its criticism of 20th-century industrial society, although these positions are similar to those in earlier novels. The plot deals with the marriage of Sir Clifford Chatterley and his wife Connie, and begins by detailing the failure of Connie to find any fulfilment or meaning in their marriage, partly through the fact that Sir Clifford is a cripple and is confined to a wheel-chair. Connie attempts to find sexual consolation elsewhere, initially and uselessly with the artist Michaelis, but, soon after, more success-fully and meaningfully with Mellors, the gamekeeper of her husband's estate. The central point of the novel is the relation-ship between Connie and Mellors, and the fulfilment each claims to find in the other.

In finding this fulfilment in each other, however, both charac-ters are simply returning to the ideas and situation of *The Rain-bow*. The problem is worked out more intensively in a different setting—that of the upper-class society in which Clifford and Connie live. Lawrence's criticism of this sort of society is bitingly accurate, and gives the novel substance. The world of Wragby (where the Chatterleys live) is empty and meaningless:

And thus far it was a life: in the void. For the rest it was non-existence. Wragby was there, the servants . . . but spectral, not really existing.   p. 62

Sir Clifford himself represents the typical sort of upper-class coldness and deadness which Lawrence so justifiably hated (the fact that he is a cripple was apparently not intended to be symbolic, but it has point):

> They were all inwardly hard and separate, and warmth to them was just bad taste. You had to get on without it and hold your own. . . . Even the smartest aristocrats had really nothing positive of their own to hold, and their rule was really a farce, not rule at all. What was the point? It was all cold nonsense.   p. 117

The similarity between this sort of class criticism and that found throughout Lawrence's work from *Daughters of the Vicar* to the late stories, *The Virgin and the Gypsy* and *St. Mawr*, is obvious. The difference, however, between Lawrence's earlier and later attitudes lies in his view of the working-class. In the early story, *Daughters of the Vicar*, Alfred Durant could symbolise those working-class qualities of warmth and sincerity to bring some sort of fulfilment to Louisa solely on the strength of them. In *The Rainbow* (Chapter XI, 'First Love') Ursula's chance meeting with the bargeman whilst she and Skrebensky are walking along the canal gives her a suggestion of a better way of life than Skrebensky can offer her, and in *Sons and Lovers* the particular virtues which Lawrence had then seen in working-class life are constantly emphasised:

> From the middle-classes one gets ideas, and from the common people—life itself, warmth.   p. 256

In *Lady Chatterley's Lover*, however, the realisation has struck home that there is no real hope of salvation in the working-class. The working-class district of Teldershall is merely the other end of the scale to the upper-class world of Wragby, and all classes are caught up in the same process of futility and ugliness:

> The car ploughed uphill through the long squalid straggle of Teversall, the blackened brick dwellings, the black slate roofs glistening their sharp edges, the mud black with coal-dust, the

pavements wet and black. It was as if dismalness had soaked through and through everything. The utter negation of natural beauty, the utter negation of the gladness of life, the utter absence of the instinct for shapely beauty which every bird and beast has, the utter death of the human intuitive faculty was appalling. The stacks of soap in the grocers' shops, the rhubarb and lemons in the green-grocers! the awful hats in the milliners! all went by ugly, ugly, ugly, followed by the plaster-and-gilt horror of the cinema with its wet picture announcements, 'A Woman's Love!', and the new big Primitive chapel, primitive enough in its stark brick and big panes of greenish and raspberry glass in the windows. The Wesleyan chapel, higher up, was of blackened brick and stood behind iron railings and blackened shrubs. The Congregational chapel, which thought itself superior, was built of rusticated sandstone and had a steeple, but not a very high one. Just beyond were the new school buildings, expensive pink brick, and gravelled playground inside iron railings, all very imposing, and mixing the suggestion of a chapel and a prison. pp. 202–3

This passage is typical of both the best and worst features of Lawrence's later prose style. The sure handling of the repetitive rhythms and the constant emphasis on the 'blackness' of the scene is Dickensian in its initial rhetorical impact, but there is a growing sense of straining after effect as the passage develops. The awful ugliness of the landscape is well conveyed, but there is too an over-emphasis which becomes too insistent in its dogmatism, and unclear in its final effect. The repetition of 'ugly' awkwardly suggests Lawrence's vagueness as to what specifically is wrong in the scene, 'the stacks of soap in the grocers' shops, the rhubarb and lemons in the greengrocers', are not in themselves 'bad' as presented, nor are they clear pictorial images of what the writer is decrying. The cinema, the churches, the school are mentioned and provide ugly daubs of colour (green, raspberry, pink) amidst the general grey blackness, but Lawrence (and Connie is here pushed into the background by the author) is too obviously angry at the scene to convey its horror fully. Soon the passage deteriorates into ranting: the sense of sureness in the initial handling of prose rhythm is strained, and the dogmatic preacher (however right he may be) takes over from the artist:

Tevershall! That was Tevershall! Merrie England! Shakespeare's England! No, but the England of to-day, as Connie had realised since she had come to live in it. It was producing a new race of mankind, over-conscious in the money and social and political side, on the spontaneous, intuitive side dead, but dead. Half-corpses all of them: but with a terrible insistent consciousness in the other half. There was something uncanny and underground about it all. It was an underworld. . . . She felt again in a wave of terror the grey, gritty hopelessness of it all. With such creatures for the industrial masses, and the upper-classes as she knew them, there was no hope, no hope any more.   pp. 203–4

The hopelessness which Connie and Lawrence feel about the situation in such a society as this is a dominant feature of the book, and it is emphasised again in the character of Mellors. He comes from the working-classes and purposely retains many of their characteristics, but he is exceptional only in his difference from them:

Yet Mellors had come out of all this!—Yes, but he was as apart from it all as she was. Even in him there was no fellowship left. It was dead. The fellowship was dead. There was only apartness and hopelessness, as far as all this was concerned. And this was England, the vast bulk of England: as Connie knew, since she had motored from the centre of it.   p. 204

It is worth emphasising that Mellors is really classless. Although of working-class origin, he had been a commissioned officer in the war. He is able to move easily from speaking 'correct' middle-class English to the local dialect. In coming to Tevershall after the war he had made a definite decision to reject middle-class values, but he is unable to find in the common people the warmth he had expected:

So, he had come back to his own class. To find there, what he had forgotten during his absence of years, a pettiness and a vulgarity of manner extremely distasteful.   p. 192

The notion of Mellors's individuality is important, because it is not out of place here to repeat that what Lawrence is doing in this novel and elsewhere is not to suggest that anything so crude as indiscriminate sex in itself can bring about salvation from the horrors of industrial society. As in *The Rainbow*, it is only a sexual relationship between special kinds of people which can bring fulfilment. Connie and Michaelis achieve nothing worthwhile, whilst Connie and Mellors, in Lawrence's eyes at least, achieve everything. The main difficulty for the reader is in accepting Mellors as a valid character for the purpose he has to serve. One feels that there is a slightly artificial conception at work in using Mellors as the gamekeeper/working-class representative to bring salvation to Connie, and the whole relationship has a slight air of incredibility which prevents it from carrying conviction as a realistic story. Both Connie and Mellors are frustrated and distorted by previous experiences, yet their peculiarity is not one which makes the positive values in their relationship so different from the relationships in *The Rainbow* or *Women in Love*.

The main difference between *Lady Chatterley's Lover* and these two earlier novels, of course, lies in its descriptions of sexual love which resulted in the novel's being banned for so long. From a literary point of view Lawrence is more successful in these descriptions in this novel than he was in many of the scenes in *Women in Love*, where the specifically sexual relations of Ursula and Birkin are described in appallingly bad and euphemistic prose. It is easy to find a certain element of ridiculousness and pretentiousness in these sections of *Lady Chatterley's Lover*, but on the whole these episodes in the novel are not without merit. In no sense of the word are they pornographic, and the reader who hopes to find them so is missing the real point of the book. Yet apart from a more intensive investigation of the nature of sexual love there is little that is entirely new in the novel. Lawrence attacks Sir Clifford Chatterley and the world he represents confidently enough and the negative criticism is compelling and forceful, but one feels that with Clifford, as with Kangaroo, or Massy (in *Daughters of the Vicar*), or Rico (in *St. Mawr*), the opposition is too simply drawn. He is too ridiculous, as in the scene with Connie where he discusses the 'life of the mind' and one of the latest pseudo-scientific/religious books which he so much admires. Lawrence makes his target too easy, and there is the same inability which we have noted in some other novels to understand the other point of view. This inability was soon to reach its most extreme point in the short tale *The Man Who Died*, in which the 'resurrected' Jesus is made aware of the two-fold realisation that he himself has been wholly wrong and Lawrence right.

All this, of course, is to ignore the better side of Lawrence's achievement in *Lady Chatterley's Lover*. Its assertive quality is brutally realistic in its social criticism, although overdone in its sexual concern. The utter hopelessness of the social world is contrasted with the love of Connie and Mellors, which takes on a poignancy from the comparison. This is well brought out by W. B. Yeats in a letter to Olivia Shakespear (22 May 1933):

> These two lovers, the gamekeeper and his employer's wife, each separated from their class by their love, and by fate, are poignant in their loneliness, and the coarse language of the one, accepted by both, becomes a forlorn poetry uniting their solitudes, something ancient, humble and terrible.

Yet this poignancy in the novel is almost accidental, and Lawrence does not develop it. Sex is stressed so vigorously that it seems to blot out the rest of the universe and to be the only island in a sea of despair. The concept of 'tenderness', or regard and respect for the other partner, which is an important element in the sexual doctrine of the novel (in fact Lawrence had thought of calling the novel *Tenderness* at one time) is not enough to make the reader feel that the novel is *completely* one of sexual normality. And because Lawrence insists so much and so stridently on the validity of sensual experience as the only meaningful escape from the hopelessness of the industrial civilisation of this century, the reader is made aware of the total lack of any tragic sense in his work. If one accepts Lawrence's view of the lovers and the antagonism of the rest of the world to them, then their situation (and perhaps ours) must be deeply tragic. Few would disagree with Connie that 'when the human being is full of courage and full of life, how beautiful it is', which seems to be one main assertion of the novel. There are factors in life, however, outside of industrial activity and class distinctions, which cause beauty and love to decay. Lawrence's vision, exceptional as it was, seemed unable to comprehend the nature of the human situation in its tragic aspects, and *Lady Chatterley's Lover* is far from being a triumphant assertion of his arrival at the end of his search for new values.

D. H. Lawrence at Kiowa, by Kai Gotzsche

6

The Short Novels and Stories

The emphasis so far given to Lawrence's major novels should not
be allowed to suggest that the shorter fiction is not interesting or
important. In fact it may well be that for some readers the real
virtue of Lawrence's work is more readily appreciable in the best
of the short stories, and it may appear from the discussion of the
novels in previous chapters that certain features of Lawrence's
achievement mentioned there—notably his ability to invest
simple episodes with an added level of symbolic meaning—are
essentially ones which a short-story writer would be able to
develop fruitfully. The method of *Sons and Lovers* and *The
Rainbow*, for example, consists of the presentation of various
episodes which are dramatically realised in themselves and which
are joined to each other like links in a chain, each link of which
could be a short story in itself. Most other novelists handle their
plots in a more obvious sequential fashion, with one event arising
naturally out of the previous one, but in Lawrence's work the
plot development is often not clear on a superficial reading and
occasionally, as a result of the author allowing his characters too
much freedom (as in *Aaron's Rod* particularly, but even *The
Rainbow* is not free of it), the plots appear slightly too loose so
that the tension flags. In his shorter fiction the genre itself allows
Lawrence's virtues full play: among the problems facing
a writer of short stories are the pressure of time, and the need to
sketch his characters quickly and tersely and yet to make them
credible. The good short-story writer must make the reader feel
that his characters have some independent existence of their own,
that they are not simply brought to life for the short duration of
the story to point a moral or adorn a tale, and at the same time

he must make both the characters and their situation interesting yet not incredible to the reader. These points are, of course, also features of the novelist's art, but the novelist has far more time at his disposal and can rely upon broader effects. At times the novelist can afford to let the interest slacken, whereas the short-story writer dare not let his tension relax and yet, without exaggeration or over-emphasis, must not give the appearance that the situation he is dealing with is over-contrived. The need to convey 'reality', so important to nearly all writers of prose fiction, is an even more complicated problem to the writer of short stories than to the novelist, in that the teller of the short story must persuade his reader that life is a series of highly-wrought incidents of which his tale is part, and yet a special part with particular significance. He must also ensure that his endings have point enough to convey this significance; for the reader to react after reading a short story by asking 'so what?' is a damning criticism of his work that is less important to a longer novelist. One can excuse a weak or anti-climactic ending in a novel if the novelist has engaged our interest in other ways in the book, but in a short story a weak ending is intolerable.

It is difficult, of course, to be precise in any meaningful sense in distinguishing a short story from a novel. In Lawrence's case the 'shorter' fiction ranges in theme and length from what are indisputably 'short' stories such as *The Christening*, through 'long' short stories such as *Daughters of the Vicar*, to works that are virtually short novels such as *St. Mawr* and *The Captain's Doll*. The only justification for including the two last-named stories in this section of the book is to say that Lawrence's major novels discussed in previous chapters do follow through certain ideas and attempt to develop these ideas from one novel to the other, whereas the shorter fiction does not *develop* these ideas in the same way. The short stories are occasionally experimental in style but are not markedly so in their ideas. The basic themes of Lawrence's work are developed in the longer novels, and the stories (whilst far from being mere surplus material left over from the novels) simply examine these themes with different emphasis of technique and do not embody major new departures.

A common theme of many of these short tales and stories is the usual Lawrentian subject of personal relationships, and these are examined in many different conventions and classes of society ranging from working-class life of the English Midlands before and during the First World War to middle- and upper-class society of post-war Germany, Austria and Mexico in the 1920s. The stories range in tone, too, from the very different types of comedy represented by two such stories as *Monkey Nuts* and *The Captain's Doll* to the seriousness and moving urgency of *Odour of Chrysanthemums* or *St. Mawr*. There will not be opportunity in the space of this chapter to account adequately for all of the short stories; rather than simply listing all of them, a representative group taken from the whole spread of Lawrence's writing career will be examined, although it should be realised that the resulting concentration, mainly on the better stories, is not to imply that all of the short fiction is of this quality. Taken as a whole, Lawrence's short fiction is as varied in quality as it is different in tone and length.

The short stories range in time of writing over the whole of Lawrence's writing career, and from the very beginning one can see from such a story as *The White Stocking* (which was originally entered in a newspaper competition in 1907) Lawrence's capability as a writer. The stories usually appeared initially in magazine form, and eventually most of them were published in the collections *The Prussian Officer* (1914); *England, My England* (1922); *The Ladybird* (1923, which included *The Fox* and *The Captain's Doll*); and *The Woman Who Rode Away* (1928). Some of the longer tales were published separately, particularly *St. Mawr* (along with *The Princess*) in 1925; *The Man Who Died* (also known as *The Escaped Cock*) in 1929; and *The Virgin and the Gypsy* posthumously in 1930.

TWO EARLY STORIES

Many of Lawrence's early stories are centred on the Nottinghamshire mining districts of his childhood, but the best of them—notably *Odour of Chrysanthemums* and *Daughters of the Vicar*—are much more than sketches of working-class life or mere surplus material from *Sons and Lovers*. *Odour of Chrysanthemums* in particular must rate as a masterpiece, and it is astonishing that Lawrence should have had the skill even at this time (the story may have been written as early as 1908, and was published in 1911) to write stories such as this, for the style and technique of the two early full-length novels contemporary with it are much less masterly. There is a well-known story, but one which bears repeating, of Ford Madox Ford's acceptance of the tale for publication in the *English Review* in 1911. Ford read only the first paragraph of *Odour of Chrysanthemums*, then immediately accepted it for publication:

> You are . . . for as long as the story lasts, to be in one of those untidy, unfinished landscapes where locomotives wander innocuously amongst women with baskets. That is to say, you are going to learn how what we used to call 'the other half'—though we might as well have said the other ninety-nine hundredths—lives. And if you are an editor and that is what you are after, you know that you have got what you want and you can pitch the story straight away into your wicker tray with the few accepted manuscripts and go on to some other occupation . . . Because this man knows. He knows how to open a story with a sentence of the right cadence for holding the attention. He knows how to construct a paragraph. He knows the life he is writing about in a landscape just sufficiently constructed with a casual word here and there. You can trust him for the rest.
>
> THE BODLEY HEAD FORD MADOX FORD, Vol. I. p. 323

One drawback to this anecdote is that its widespread currency has tended to focus the reader's admiration on to the opening paragraph rather than on to the tale as a whole. What is needed also is to emphasise the fact that the usual Lawrentian contrast between nature and industry is well made in the opening section of the story, for it is the unpleasant atmosphere of the tainted world of nature which is most remarkably evoked. 'The fields were dreary and forsaken', and both the countryside and the mining cottage are spoilt by the onrush of industry:

> A large bony vine clutched at the house, as if to claw down the tiled roof. Round the brick yard grew a few wintry primroses.

Beyond, the long garden sloped down to a bush-covered brook course. There were some twiggy apple trees, winter-crack trees, chrysanthemums, like pink cloths hung on bushes.

THE COMPLETE SHORT STORIES, Vol. II, pp. 283-4

The hardness and bitterness of Elizabeth Bates, the central woman of the tale, is well led up to by this initial description. The story concerns the domestic situation of the Bates family and the strained and awkward relationship of the man and wife, although the husband never comes before us until he is dead, killed in a mining accident. The situation is simple enough, and the mining accident a stereotype of a thousand similar stories of mining villages, but Lawrence invests the situation with a deep and moving significance. In the first part of the tale the tension and harshness of the household is well built up as the rest of the family wait for the husband to return from work, but it is assumed that he has once more gone straight from work to the public house; in the second part the tone changes, with the tension switching to a different key as the husband's continued absence becomes more ominous. Eventually he is brought home dead, and the fact of his death throws into another perspective the lives of the man's wife and mother. The tone is perfectly caught, for the miner's death is not sentimentalised over; rather, the wife, Elizabeth, is made aware of the transitoriness of life and her own past error in allowing the ordinariness and mundaneness of her lot to stifle her feelings and demean her character. Now he is dead she realises with tragic immediacy the fact that he was different from her and different from her conception of him:

> Life with its smoky burning gone from him, had left him apart, and utterly alien to her. And she knew what a stranger he was to her. In her womb was ice of fear, because of this separate stranger with whom she had been living as one flesh. Was this what it all meant—utter, intact separateness, obscured by heat of living? In dread she turned her face away. . . . For as she looked at the dead man, her mind, cold and detached, said clearly: 'Who am I? What have I been doing? I have been fighting a husband who did not exist. *He* existed all the time. What wrong have I done? What was

that I have been living with? There lies the reality, this man.' And her soul died in her for fear: she knew that she had never seen him, he had never seen her, they had met in the dark and had fought in the dark, not knowing whom they met nor whom they fought. And now she saw, and turned silent in seeing. For she had been wrong.   pp. 300–1

The passage is interesting, not only in that it shows Lawrence's own awareness of the fact of death, but also in its effect in the story as a whole. The 'ice of fear' in her 'womb' (a word so annoying to some readers of Lawrence, not always without cause) here is effectually used to cast the reader's mind back to a previous scene where the contrast of life and death, and the meanness of the woman in her 'death-in-life', is well shown when, as she reaches up to light the lamp, her daughter remarks at the chrysanthemums which she had earlier placed in her apron-band. The parallel between her wearing the flowers and her pregnancy is symbolic of life:

> As she reached up, her figure displayed itself just rounding with maternity.
> 'Oh, mother—!' exclaimed the girl.
> 'What?' said the woman, suspended in the act of putting the lamp-glass over the flame. The copper reflector shone handsomely on her, as she stood with uplifted arm, turning to face her daughter.
> 'You've got a flower in your apron!' said the child, in a little rapture at this unusual event.
> 'Goodness me!' exclaimed the woman, relieved. 'One would have thought the house was afire.' She replaced the glass and waited a moment before turning up the wick. A pale shadow was seen floating vaguely on the floor.
> 'Let me smell!' said the child, still rapturously, coming forward and putting her face to her mother's waist.
> 'Go along, silly!' said the mother, turning up the lamp. The light revealed their suspense so that the woman found it almost unbearable. Annie was still bending at her waist. Irritably, the mother took the flowers out from her apron-band.
> 'Oh, mother—don't take them out!' Annie cried, catching her hand and trying to replace the sprig.
> 'Such nonsense!' said the mother, turning away.   pp. 288–9

The symbolism of the scene is wonderfully suggestive of the child's delight in life and the mother's dismissal of it, and it is remarkable that the symbolism Lawrence is employing here to parallel the flowers and the woman's pregnancy is typical of the symbolism of many English folk songs, such as 'The Seeds of Love'; Lawrence may well have been writing consciously or unconsciously in a folk-convention at this point. (It is not out of place to remind ourselves that Lawrence is one of the first writers in English of truly working-class origins.) However, Lawrence is not perfect in his handling of this scene, for although it is beautifully formed as it is quoted above, its effect is slightly spoilt by the way in which one aspect of its significance is hammered home in the next few lines, in which the woman's conscious antipathy to the flowers is shown:

> 'It was chrysanthemums when I married him, and chrysanthemums when you were born, and the first time they ever brought him home drunk, he'd got brown chrysanthemums in his buttonhole.'
>
> p. 289

The story as a whole, however, is near-faultless, and is one of the best possible introductions to Lawrence's work.

Daughters of the Vicar (which was probably written after *Odour of Chrysanthemums* and certainly by September 1911) has received much praise in the past from critics, but one wonders how much of this praise is due to the nature of its social comment as distinct from its literary virtue. The story is certainly not without merit, but there is an element of naïvety in its suggestion of working-class 'life' significantly opposed to the sterility of the middle-class world of the vicarage. The plot concerns the two daughters, Mary and Louisa, of the Reverend Ernest Lindley, and their marriages: Mary marries the Reverend Massy, within her own class and station, and lives a life that is respectable but sterile and degrading; Louisa, the younger daughter, is at the end of the story about to marry Alfred Durant, a miner and ex-sailor; and Lawrence suggests that she has made the finer choice. Certainly, as the issue is presented, Mary's marriage to Massy is shown as something to be wholeheartedly deplored, and the contrast between Massy and Alfred Durant leaves no doubt of the miner's superiority. Yet this superiority is due more to the unpleasantness of Massy rather than to any marked characteristic in Alfred, and a weakness of the tale lies in the way in which Massy is caricatured. To his mother-in-law Massy is an 'abortion', unprepossessing in appearance, and Lawrence loads the case against him:

> His most irritating habit was that of a sneering little giggle, all on his own, which came when he perceived or related some illogical absurdity on the part of another person. . . . In normal human relationship he was not there. Quite unable to take part in simple everyday talk, he padded silently round the house, or sat in the dining-room looking nervously from side to side, always apart in a cold, rarefied little world of his own. Sometimes he made an ironic remark, that did not seem humanly relevant, or he gave his little laugh, like a sneer.
>
> THE COMPLETE SHORT STORIES, Vol. I, pp. 145–6

As caricature this is cleverly done, and one gathers from this excerpt all those features of Massy's character—his smallness, his sneer, his 'padding' about like something inhuman—which Lawrence wishes to suggest; but as a serious characterisation of a 'real' person it is less convincing. Many previous commentators have stressed Massy's similarity to Casaubon in George Eliot's *Middlemarch* (and Mary's faint similarity to Dorothea in the same novel), but the comparison only serves to underline the relative awkwardness of Lawrence's character.

This is not to say that the portrayal of life at the vicarage as a whole and of the middle-class snobbery of the Lindleys is not forcefully or meaningfully presented, for as Dr. Leavis has commented (and Dr. Leavis's praise of the story cannot be lightly dismissed): 'The pride of class-superiority—and class at the vicarage . . . appears as the enemy of life, starving and thwarting and denying, and breeding in consequence hate and ugliness' (*D. H. Lawrence: Novelist*, London, 1955, p. 75). In its attack on 'the pride of class-superiority' the story is devastating, apart from the characterisation of Massy, but the tale is weaker in its presentation of the values of working-class life which are shown with a touch of idealisation. This 'idealisation' does not lie, of course, in any attempt to emphasise the richness and importance of life in the Durants' cottage contrasted with the deadness of the vicarage, for the cottage is shown from the start in an unfavourable light in the rudeness of both of Alfred's parents to the Reverend Lindley when he visits them, and there is an equally unattractive scene later when Massy and Louisa visit Mr. Durant on his death-bed. The 'idealisation' lies rather in the naïvety with which it is suggested that the values of the world of the Durants are, *in some way which is not properly developed*, meaningful ones which can give some fulfilment to Louisa through her love for Alfred. This is certainly not to deny that these values could not be meaningful, but simply to suggest that Lawrence does not develop them convincingly enough in the tale, for it is unconvincing to imply that Louisa could have felt them simply by washing Alfred's back free of coal-grime.

The failure to develop completely acceptable reasons why Alfred brings some salvation to Louisa is paralleled too by a failure to develop another important theme raised in *Daughters of the Vicar*, namely Alfred's shyness and suggested impotency in his relations with women. This aspect of the tale has often been ignored by previous commentators, but Alfred's inability to establish any proper relationship with women is brought up by Lawrence on two or three occasions, and presumably Louisa is meant to restore Alfred to a sense of the meaning of life as much as he is meant to restore her. The impotency theme is one which recurs curiously often in some of Lawrence's short stories, and the fact that is never adequately handled is of some interest. In *Daughters of the Vicar* the theme is left undefined, and the lack of development of these major features is a drawback to what is otherwise an interesting and highly characteristic story.

'TICKETS PLEASE' AND 'MONKEY-NUTS'

Lawrence's Comic Sense

These two stories date from the end of the First World War and are noteworthy in that they deal with relationships between the sexes in terms of comedy and of the 'sex-war', although *Tickets*

Please certainly has other undertones. Comedy is not usually associated with Lawrence's major novels, but several short stories (and many of the satirical poems, as we shall see in the next chapter) reveal Lawrence in a more relaxed mood.

Tickets Please deals with the conductresses and the inspector of the tramway service. Because of the absence of most of the men of the district, who are in the services and away fighting, the trams are run mainly by women, and John Thomas Raynor, the chief inspector, is able to indulge his flirtatious and amorous tendencies with a wide selection of young women. The inspector's two christian names, and his nickname of 'Coddy', are (or were) familiar slang terms for what Lawrence is only vaguely disguising in his character: Raynor is the aggressive, good-looking male seeking and taking his pleasure where he can find it. The girls on the tram-service decide to teach him a lesson and attempt to force him to 'go steady' with one of them, but the story, which starts off light-heartedly enough, ends in a different note and reveals a crueller, perverse element in the girls' attitude.

A feature of the tale which links up with Lawrence's other work is the repeated contrast of light and darkness made in it: the trams are a haven of refuge, brightly lit and warm, as opposed to the darkness outside. In Lawrence's other work the contrast, however, is made more seriously, for it is in the outer darkness that 'reality' lies; in *Tickets Please* the contrast is comic:

> It is quite common for a car, packed with one solid mass of living people, to come to a dead halt in the midst of unbroken blackness, the heart of nowhere on a dark night, and for the driver and the girl conductor to call: 'All get off—car's on fire!' Instead, however, of rushing out in panic, the passengers stolidly reply: 'Get on—get on! We're stopping where we are. Push on, George.' So till flames actually appear.   THE COMPLETE SHORT STORIES, Vol. II, pp. 334–5

The darkness is a good place for the inspector to walk into with his current girl-friend, and in the cinema too the comic mood is caught when 'during these performances pitch darkness falls from time to time, when the machine goes wrong. Then there is a wild whooping, and a loud smacking of simulated kisses.

(p. 338). The comedy, however, is not sustained. When the girls trap the inspector in their waiting-room and attempt to make him choose one of them as a permanent lover they begin, 'more in fun than in spite or anger', to hit and pummel him, but the true nature of their feelings of antagonism soon breaks through, and the story ends on a sombre note with the comic mask of the tale being slipped off to reveal more basic feelings underneath.

In *Monkey-Nuts* the comic mood is sustained throughout, but again, as in *Tickets Please*, the comedy is allied with a real human situation. Two soldiers, Albert the corporal, and Joe, a private, are posted to a small village to help supervise the goods handling at the railway station. A land-girl, Miss Stokes, brings a hay-cart to the sidings, and although it is Albert who is loquacious and interested in flirting with her, she becomes interested only in the shy, retiring Joe, and sets about getting him as directly as she can. The comic note is struck from her first appearance, for she is cold to Albert's flirtations:

> 'Now that's the wagoner for us, boys,' said the corporal loudly.
> 'Whoa!' she said to her horses; and then to the corporal: 'Which boys do you mean?'
> 'We are the pick of the bunch. That's Joe, my pal. Don't you let on that my name's Albert,' said the corporal to his private. 'I'm the corporal.'
> 'And I'm Miss Stokes,' said the land-girl coolly, 'if that's all the boys you are.'   p. 367

However, she soon begins setting her cap at Joe, inviting him by telegram to meet her in town, an invitation he ignores. The triangular situation is amusingly handled with Miss Stokes pursuing Joe, and Albert Miss Stokes, but all Albert gets for his witticisms and advances is the straightforward colloquialism: 'Monkey nuts!' or a direct invitation to lose himself. Joe is all but forced to carry out his assignations with the land-girl, which he does sullenly and with bad grace. His resentment at her behaviour deepens the realism of the story, and eventually Albert goes to one of the assignations in Joe's place, explaining with little tact when he meets her: Joe 'is not conducting the service tonight:

he asked me if I'd officiate' (p. 377). Albert's support gives Joe enough courage to resist the advances of the predatory female, for when she calls out to him the following day he is able to reply 'Monkey nuts!' to her demands. She comes no more to the siding—'and Joe felt more relieved even than he had felt when he heard the firing cease, after the news had come that the armistice was signed'.

'THE CAPTAIN'S DOLL'

Monkey-Nuts is a relatively slight although amusing sketch of sexual relationships. *The Captain's Doll* is a much longer and more substantial work in which the comic mood is handled in yet a different way again, for the story is set in a middle- to upper-class environment in occupied Germany and details the relationship between Alexander Hepburn, a Scottish officer, and Hannele, a German aristocrat fallen on hard times, who makes a living creating dolls. The doll she makes in Hepburn's image is at once both a caricature and a symbol of him, for in spite of his having an affair with Hannele he keeps himself detached and objective in his refusal to tell his wife in Britain of it, or to give Hannele any indication of the exact nature of his feelings or his future plans. He is pleasant and well-meaning, but infuriatingly vague, and his indecision is amusingly captured in the first few pages of the story. Hannele has to cross-examine him to get the simplest admissions of his feelings: does he want to go back to visit his wife?—does he want to remain in Germany? Hepburn remains vague yet pleasant to all her questions, but the surprising virtue of his characterisation is the way in which Lawrence makes him *real* for all his vagueness and doll-like ingenuousness.

The finest comedy in the story, and possibly the best humorous scene in Lawrence's fiction, is the arrival of Hepburn's wife from England and her conversation with Hannele about him. For a start Mrs. Hepburn mistakes Hannele's sister Mitchka for her husband's lover, and invites Hannele herself to tea in order to get her to warn her sister away from Hepburn. The ensuing conversation is a brilliant *tour de force*—the 'little woman' sets off on a preposterous speech in which her sexual values are amusingly satirised, and is so unwittingly frank that Hannele has to 'put her fingers to her ears, to make sure they were not falling off' at what she hears. Mrs. Hepburn's values of married life are what Lawrence himself was attacking so much more seriously in his major novels:

> 'Why, I had a friend in Ireland. She and her husband had been an ideal couple, an *ideal* couple. Real playmates. And you can't say more than that, can you?'
>
> THE SHORT NOVELS, Vol. I., 'The Captain's Doll', p. 27

Mrs. Hepburn's view of her husband's married perfection is made almost incredible to Hannele by the remark of his behaviour on their wedding night, when 'he kneeled down in front of me and promised, with God's help, to make my life happy' (p. 28). This reminiscence unseats Hannele's affection for Hepburn far more than the malicious undertones which become more apparent as the 'little lady' goes on, for as Hannele later recollects:

> Of course if he had been at her own feet, then Hannele would have thought it almost natural: almost a necessary part of the show of love. But at the feet of that other little woman! And what was that other little woman wearing? Her wedding night! Hannele hoped before heaven it wasn't some awful little nighty of frail flowered silk. Imagine it, that little lady! Perhaps in a chic little boudoir cap of punto di Milano, and this slip of frail flowered silk: and the man, perhaps, in his braces! Oh, merciful heaven, save us from other people's indiscretions. No, let us be sure it was in proper evening dress—twenty years ago—very low cut, with a full skirt gathered behind and trailing a little, and a little feather-erection in her high-dressed hair, and all those jewels: pearls of course: and he in a dinner-jacket and a white waistcoat: probably in an hotel bedroom in Lugano, or Biarritz. And she? Was she standing with one small hand on his shoulder? Or was she seated on the couch in the bedroom? Oh, dreadful thought! And yet, it was almost inevitable, that scene. Hannele had never been married, but she had come quite near enough to the realisation of the event to know that such a scene *was* practically inevitable. An indispensable part of any honeymoon. Him on his knees, with his heels up!

And how black and tidy his hair must have been then! And no

grey at the temples at all. Such a good-looking bridegroom. Perhaps with a white rose in his button-hole still. And she could see him kneeling there, in his new black trousers, and a wing collar. And she could see his head bowed. And she could hear his plangent, musical voice saying: 'With God's help, I will make your life happy. I will live for that and for nothing else.' And then the little lady must have had tears in her eyes, and she must have said, rather superbly: 'Thank you, dear. I'm perfectly sure of it.'

pp. 34-5

The story cannot sustain the comedy, however, and it deteriorates slightly after Mrs. Hepburn is very clumsily removed from the plot when she dies falling out of a hotel window. Hepburn and Hannele lose touch with each other, and when, later in the story, Hepburn returns to look for Hannele his character has changed so that he at times bears an uncomfortable similarity to Birkin in *Women in Love*. The latter part of the story is in one sense a debate on love and marriage carried on half-seriously and half-comically by Lawrence. The characters of both Hannele and Hepburn are criticised to a certain degree, but the pace falters as Lawrence seems to be investing Hepburn, the 'doll' of the earlier part of the story, with a significant insight into the problems of love and marriage which he cannot convincingly carry.

'THE FOX'

The Captain's Doll appeared originally along with *The Fox* and *The Ladybird* in one collection, and curiously enough Lawrence himself approved more highly of *The Ladybird* than either of the other tales—an opinion which is hardly likely to be shared by many other readers. A feature of Lawrence's short stories from the later years of the war onwards is an underlying interest in perversity and cruelty which, however much admirers of Lawrence's work would wish to play down, must be taken into account in any general evaluation of his work. *The Fox*, for example, is one of Lawrence's greatest stories: characterisation is vivid, the tension hardly flags, and symbolism is used with magnificent force to point one of the story's themes. Yet at the same time there is an uneasiness as to exactly what Lawrence's attitude is towards the story he is telling. The plot concerns two young women who run a chicken farm, not very successfully, and a young man who returns from the war and interrupts their domestic contentment. The two girls, March and Banford, are satisfied with each other's company, and there is more than a suggestion of a lesbian, though non-physical, relationship between them; but when the man, Henry Grenfel, arrives, the relationship between the two girls is strained by Henry's interest in March and hers in him. The girls' covert lesbianism is nowhere openly recognised by them or by the intruder (later in the story Henry's antagonism towards Banford is brought out—'I hope you'll be paid back for all the harm you've done me for nothing.' In terms of the real nature of the girls' relationship it is hardly 'for nothing').

The symbolism of the tale gives point to the whole situation. The early attention given in the story to a fox attacking the girls' chickens is obviously used as an image of the real nature of the situation between the three central characters: Henry is the fox, the hunter, the intruder taking what he wants. In this sense it is temptingly easy to read Henry as some kind of Lawrentian hero, rescuing March from the unnatural relationship with Banford, but such a reading would be quite false as the story starts. Henry has much in common with Annable of *The White Peacock*, and his similarity to the fox is not admirable. His interest in March is nowhere properly defined; it is simply encouraged by Banford's hostility and uneasiness: it is cold, calculated desire, and in this respect he hardly has Lawrence's approval. At other times Lawrence gives him a measure of sympathy, particularly in the episode where he stalks and kills the real fox:

> It seemed to him it would be the last of the foxes in this loudly barking, thick-voiced England, tight with innumerable little houses.
> THE SHORT NOVELS, Vol. I, 'The Fox', p. 36

On the whole, however, it is difficult to be sure of how Henry is to be regarded, and as his reasons for wanting March are left vague, so the final episode of the story becomes the more horrifying: he chops down a tree knowing that it will fall on Banford, and so kills her. He has removed his rival and so wins March for himself, but the end of the tale discloses a world of completely amoral values. There is no real suggestion that March is better in exchanging Banford for him, and indeed her final mood is one of drifting hopelessness which brings her into the world peopled by many of Lawrence's heroines in the shorter fiction, of Lou and Mrs. Witt in *St. Mawr*, of the Woman Who Rode Away, of Yvette in *The Virgin and the Gypsy*:

> Poor March, in her goodwill and her responsibility, she had strained herself till it seemed to her that the whole of life and everything was only a horrible abyss of nothingness. The more you reached after the fatal flower of happiness, which trembles so blue and lovely in a crevice just beyond your grasp, the more fearfully you become aware of the ghastly and awful gulf of the precipice below you, into which you will inevitably plunge, as into the bottomless pit, if you reach any further.   p. 67

'ST. MAWR' AND THE LATER STORIES

Many of the later stories, for all their occasional power, leave the reader with a sense of unease and dissatisfaction. Great literature, of course, often causes us to question and challenge our own values, and often we are uneasy on first reading a poem or novel because we are unwilling to allow our feelings to be altered from their set mould; but in the case of these later stories the sense of exasperation and disquiet is not wholly the fault of the reader. Lawrence's tremendous genius is apparent in many of them, and parts of *St. Mawr* and *The Virgin and the Gypsy* are in their own ways brilliantly handled, but the power of the writing is often curiously muted by the extreme positions of virulence and perversity which afflict them at various points. It has been suggested in the previous discussion of the major novels that Lawrence did not fruitfully develop his basic ideas after the writing of *The Rainbow* and *Women in Love*, and the faults apparent in the novels succeeding these two are often the faults of the later stories as well. The short stories are also, however, at the same time more experimental and yet more relaxed than the novels, and as a result

Lawrence often writes himself into situations which are strained and even, occasionally, quite ludicrous.

St. Mawr is notable in many respects as one of the most important of the shorter tales, and some of the writing is of a high quality, particularly in the descriptions and evocations of the Texas and Arizona countryside. It is not out of order here to remind the reader of one aspect of Lawrence's writing—his travel books—which we have not space to discuss properly in this study, for one of Lawrence's great and indisputable virtues is his ability to evoke a sense of place. The story itself, however, is engaged with much deeper issues than this simple evocation, for its theme is the typical one of the individual's sense of meaninglessness in the midst of so-called civilised English society and her attempt to establish some pattern of sense and meaning in life by withdrawing to an isolated ranch in New Mexico. The heroine, Lou Witt, is married to Rico, a society playboy (supposedly but implausibly meant to be Australian), but life with him is empty and ugly. The artificial world in which they live is similar to that drawn in *Lady Chatterley's Lover*, and is forcefully presented by Lawrence in spite of the fact that such a situation was now becoming stereotyped in his work; but a new element is introduced by St. Mawr, a horse which Lou buys for Rico and which becomes for her an indication and a symbol of a finer, more significant world.

The significance which Lou attaches to St. Mawr is no doubt a weakness in the story, and is awkwardly handled by Lawrence (it is noteworthy that the horse is hardly mentioned in the final, most compelling pages of the tale). One does not want to dwell on the 'ancient understanding' which seems to 'flood in' to her 'weary young-woman's soul' when first she sees the horse, and this and the over-insistence on the intuitive awareness of life which both the horse and Lewis, its Welsh and 'lost-Faery-world-forlorn' groom, possess are radical weaknesses which can hardly be justified. The concept that they, like the gypsy in *The Virgin and the Gypsy* or the primitive Indians in *The Woman Who Rode Away*, possess some markedly undefined understanding of the significance of life is too naïve to be convincing, at least in the terms in which they are shown within the narrow limits of a short story. What is convincing and deeply moving in the story is the urgency with which Lou's sense of desperation with the uselessness and emptiness of the 'civilisation' in which she lives is conveyed, an urgency which is so compelling that even Dr. Leavis's comparison of the tale with T. S. Eliot's *The Waste Land* seems praise too slight for it. 'I want the wonder back again, or I shall die' is Lou's appeal, and it is exactly its ruthless analysis of modern society and Lou's predicament in it, living and partly living in futile sequence a life which lacks wonder or meaning, which makes *St. Mawr* worth reading for all its faults.

St. Mawr, for all its unevenness, is amongst the most interesting and important of Lawrence's works, although like *The Woman Who Rode Away*, another noteworthy tale based on his experiences in the United States and Mexico, it suffers from a certain ingenuous vagueness in stating its positive values. Of the other later short stories, *The Virgin and the Gypsy* stands out, although some critics have found much to admire in two very different experimental tales—the satirical *The Man Who Loved Islands* and the controversial *The Man Who Died*. Little needs to be said here about *The Virgin and the Gypsy*, for it follows the usual Lawrentian pattern of the young woman bored with the artificiality and futility of her middle-class existence, although the satirical portrait of her family situation, with her selfish and unpleasant grandmother presiding over the family like 'some great red-blotched fungus', is a compelling reworking of the kind of attack on middle-class family life that is central to so early a story as *Daughters of the Vicar*. *The Man Who Died*, however, is a story quite different from anything else Lawrence wrote, and here again the reader may well experience that sense of disquiet over some aspects of Lawrence's experimentalisation to which attention has already been drawn in discussing *The Fox* and *St. Mawr*.

The Man Who Died is obviously disquieting to some readers in that it deals with one of the central tenets of Christian civilisation and alters this tenet to fit in with Lawrence's own scheme of values. The central figure of the tale (the Man who died) is

Christ, who in Lawrence's own words, at the time of the Resurrection:

> gets up and feels very sick about everything, and can't stand the old crowd any more—so cuts out—and as he heals up, he begins to find what an astonishing place the phenomenal world is, far more marvellous than any salvation or heaven—and thanks his stars he needn't have a 'mission' any more.
>
> Letter to Earl Brewster, 3 May 1927

The story is unsatisfactory, however, in more important ways than its tampering with traditional religious attitudes, for it raises directly the whole problem of Lawrence's failure to understand Christianity, and the attempt to reinterpret the resurrected Christ as a Lawrentian hero merely ends in banality, in spite of the confident serenity of the prose style. Whatever one's own view of Christianity, Lawrence's insistence on the significance and meaning the resurrected Christ sees in the beauty and vitality of the 'phenomenal' world of nature around him, for all its appeal, so obviously ignores other issues of existence. Lawrence's world, for good or ill, is one in which the overpowering beauty of nature overshadows all other values, and in *The Man Who Died* Christ is concerned not with moral questions of good or evil but with developing an aesthetic response to that world both through contemplation of it and in the sexual relationship with the priestess of Isis. The nature of this aesthetic response is expressed in the story in terms which many readers, and not only Christian ones, will feel to be laboured and untypical of the author of *Odour of Chrysanthemums*.

7

Lawrence's Poetry

This study of Lawrence's work has concerned itself almost entirely with his prose fiction, and it is certainly as a writer in this genre that his real virtues lie. He did, however, interest himself in other forms of artistic expression: as a dramatist, as an artist, as a writer of fine travel books, as a literary and social critic and essayist, and as a poet: but his ability in these fields is varied, and only the criticism and the travel books can be wholeheartedly recommended as typical of the best of his achievement. Lawrence wrote his plays largely as a relaxation from writing fiction, although one play in particular—*The Daughter-in-Law*—is excellent and has been successfully staged in London. It is with Lawrence as a poet, however, that we must conclude our examination of his work.

Lawrence's poetry has been the subject of a great deal of controversy by critics who are divided about the nature of his ability in this genre. With some notable exceptions, however, it is fair to say that Lawrence is not regarded by many readers as a great poet, and indeed it is likely that if he had never written any novels and only his poems survived then his reputation as a poet would have been a minor one. Yet there are a number of interesting poems written by Lawrence, and one or two which are of considerable merit. Lawrence's poetry tends to improve as his writing career progresses, at a time when his fiction begins to become slightly repetitious and less forceful during the 1920s. The trouble with Lawrence's verse is that he himself has not the poet's proper interest in the technique of poetry. W. H. Auden has remarked that a poet 'is, before anything else, a person who is passionately in love with language', and has added that one should ask a prospective young poet why he wants to write poetry:

> If the young man answers: 'I have important things I want to say,' then he is not a poet. If he answers: 'I like hanging around words listening to what they say,' then maybe he is going to be a poet.

Auden's view, of course, might be challenged by some other poets (such as Blake, in particular) but the remark does pin-point one area of Lawrence's weakness as a poet. With Lawrence one feels too often that he is writing because he 'has things to say' rather than because of any fascinated interest in the use of words or rhythms. Certainly Lawrence has a gift for occasionally striking imagery, but his verse as a whole is often weakened by looseness of rhythms, and many poems fail to hold together as units. In his best poems, it is true, Lawrence does achieve some measure of verbal concentration, but these good poems are isolated and random, and only serve to emphasise the relative slackness of much else of the verse. Lawrence considered himself a 'modern' poet dealing with 'contemporary' issues, but his relative lack of interest in form and rhythm does cut him off markedly from those other poets around the period of the First World War and afterwards who were establishing and developing the 'modern' poetic idiom. Ezra Pound, T. S. Eliot, and Wallace Stevens were profoundly concerned with the problems and difficulties facing the poet in the 20th century, at a time when the state of the English language was not adequate to express the feelings they were struggling to define, and it was through their experimental and at times extremely complicated use of free verse techniques that 'modern' poetry emerged. Lawrence's interest in these poetic experimentations was slight, and in spite of the care with which he is known to have revised and worked on some of his poems his use of free verse techniques is often amateurish. In a famous and important essay on Lawrence's poetry, R. P. Blackmur has complained of the fallacy inherent in Lawrence's attitude to writing poetry, an attitude which arises out of the belief that the poet's feelings must be set down so spontaneously and must depend so entirely upon the demon of inspiration that the form of the poem will emerge naturally from the force of the emotion struggling to be expressed: 'that is the fallacy of expressive form . . . that if a thing is only intensely enough felt its mere expression in words will give it satisfactory form' ('D. H. Lawrence and Expressive Form' in *Language as Gesture*, N.Y., 1952, p. 289). Blackmur argues convincingly against this notion, and perceptively outlines the main weaknesses of Lawrence's verse, the problem of form and rhythm and the quality of the feelings expressed, whilst at the same time he preserves the real virtues in this verse.

EARLY POETRY

Lawrence is not a poet who was seriously interested in the poetic experiments of his own time, and his early poetry in particular is written very much under the influence of Thomas Hardy. Dylan Thomas has said of 20th-century poetry that he much preferred the bus which Hardy missed to the one that most 20th-century poets caught, and it is true that Hardy's poetry, with its brilliant evocations of nostalgia and lament for the transitoriness of life and human love, is moving in a way unequalled by any other English poet for all its apparent clumsiness of technique. There are a number of features which Lawrence's early poetry has in common with Hardy's: the use of the ballad form and local dialect, the interest in the world of nature and a detailed and precise honesty of observation of it, and an extraordinary sensitivity of feeling. On the whole, Lawrence's use of ballad metres and of local dialect is unsatisfactory (in the 'Whether or Not' sequence, pp. 76–85, for example) and this use of folk material is artificial rather than genuine. Where Lawrence's virtues are most importantly similar to Hardy's, however, and where these virtues often appear to the uninformed reader as merely sentimental and embarrassing, is in the sensitivity of feeling evoked in some of these early poems.

It is a feature too of Hardy's poetry that he verges close to the edge of sentimentality (and in his less successful poems fails lamentably to stay out of it), and in a poem such as 'Afterwards', although the borderline between genuine emotion and sentimentality is difficult to preserve, the distinction is achieved: the poem never quite becomes sentimental. A similar tendency is seen in the early *Rhyming Poems*, and in the best of them the focus on some real aspect of feeling and the sensitivity evoked should not be too hostilely rejected. It would be wrong to suggest that in 'Baby Running Barefoot' or 'End of Another Home Holiday' the feeling is clumsily handled, although it is true that the latter poem, where the nostalgia is vividly realised, is confused and over-long: the confusion, however, relates to a technical failure in the craftsmanship of the poem rather than to any lack of genuine feeling. In some poems where the evidence suggests that Lawrence has taken serious interest in compressing and reworking the earlier and looser version, such as in 'Piano', the final published poem has appeal and force which many of the other early poems lack.

'Piano' is a good example of Lawrence's rhyming poetry at its best, and brings out these problems of apparent sentimentality which the reader needs to face. This final published version did not appear until the publication of Lawrence's volume *New Poems* in 1918 and is therefore probably composed much later than many of the other *Rhyming Poems*. It evokes a mood of nostalgia and reminiscence which should not be too hastily dismissed as sentimentality:

> Softly, in the dusk, a woman is singing to me;
> Taking me back down the vista of years, till I see
> A child sitting under the piano, in the boom of the tingling strings
> And pressing the small, poised feet of a mother who smiles as she
> sings.
>
> In spite of myself, the insidious mastery of song
> Betrays me back, till the heart of me weeps to belong
> To the old Sunday evenings at home, with winter outside
> And hymns in the cosy parlour, the tinkling piano our guide.
>
> So now it is vain for the singer to burst into clamour
> With the great black piano appassionato. The glamour
> Of childish days is upon me, my manhood is cast
> Down in the flood of remembrance, I weep like a child for the past.

p. 148

The poem may well make readers new to it feel uncomfortable, but the feelings it stirs may be far more genuine than they first appear to be. The problems with a poem of this type, which deliberately arouses our sensitivity on an easily understandable feeling of nostalgia for lost childhood, is that the reader may well react to it uncritically by mistaking his stock responses for rational judgment. 'Piano' is one of the poems used by I. A. Richards as an exercise in *Practical Criticism*, in which he quotes the evaluations of the poem made by a number of his students at Cambridge in the 1920s. These evaluations are of enormous interest to anyone interested in the problems of reading poetry in general, as well as to those interested in Lawrence: so many of the criticisms of the poem which Richards quotes are obviously the result of irrational, largely unconscious, prejudices on the part of the readers about their own childhood (which they may or may not wish to remember), motherhood, the singing of hymns, that only rarely is *the poem itself* actually read with any thoroughness. So many readers of the poem seem afraid of the emotions generated by it that they do not or cannot read it with any insight, and it is only those readers who are prepared to read closely and struggle with the feeling in it who can perceive the artistic skill and control which prevents the poem from being crudely and sloppily sentimental and which makes it instead a moving poetic experience.

'PANSIES' AND 'NETTLES'

If Lawrence's early verse is written partly under the shadow of Hardy there is also an occasional suggestion of laconic wit in some of his observations (in 'After the Opera') which becomes most marked in the later volumes *Pansies* (published in 1929), *Nettles* (in 1930) and *More Pansies* (in *Last Poems*, published posthumously in 1932). The verse in these volumes cannot, of course, be taken wholly seriously as major poetry, but the terse humour and epigrammatic quality of the wit should certainly be considered in any account of Lawrence's work. The picture of the spleen-filled, misanthropic, brooding prophet-in-exile, which is how some critics see Lawrence in the last ten years of his life, is humanised by a reading of these satirical poems, and certainly Lawrence's humour, which has already been touched on in relation to the short stories, is an important facet of Lawrence the man. No doubt this humour is at times cheap and vindictive, but at other times it is magnificent. In 'Nottingham's New University', for example (overseas readers might need to be told that Boot's is a large chain-store of dispensing chemists with branches in every English town, and that the founder of the store helped to established Nottingham University College):

In Nottingham, that dismal town
where I went to school and college,
they've built a new university
for a new dispensation of knowledge.

Built it most grand and cakeily
out of the noble loot
derived from shrewd cash-chemistry
by good Sir Jesse Boot.

Little I thought when I was a lad
and turned my modest penny
over on Boot's Cash Chemist's counter,
that Jesse, by turning many

millions of similar honest pence
over, would make a pile
that would rise at last and blossom out
in grand and cakey style

into a university
where smart men would dispense
doses of smart cash-chemistry
in language of common-sense!

That future Nottingham lads would be
cash chemically B.Sc.
that Nottingham lights would rise and say:
—By Boots I am M.A.

For this I learn, though I knew it before
that culture has her roots
in the deep dung of cash, and lore
is a last offshoot of Boots.

THE COMPLETE POEMS, p. 488

The right tone here is superbly caught (whereas another version of the same poem, 'In Nottingham', p. 950 of *The Complete Poems*, completely misses its target by being too shrill and vindictive) and diction and rhythm combine to dramatise the wit.

The two *Pansies* groups of poems contain work of very differing quality and seriousness. At times some of these poems illustrate neatly some of Lawrence's main ideas: his views on sex and love, for example, are brought out by poems such as 'In a Spanish Tram-Car' (p. 617) to which reference was made in Chapter 2, 'True Love at Last' (p. 605), 'Sphinx' and 'Intimates' (p. 604). Another major theme in this group is the attack upon modern mechanical civilisation and the devotion to money which is so central a feature of this civilisation, and although the tone of some of these poems is too shrill to be convincing, at other times, as in 'Let Us Be Men', the verse has a moving force:

> For God's sake, let us be men
> not monkeys minding machines
> or sitting with our tails curled
> while the machine amuses us, the radio or film or gramophone.
>
> Monkeys with a bland grin on our faces.—

p. 450

'BIRDS, BEASTS AND FLOWERS' and 'LAST POEMS'

Lawrence's main serious poetic achievement lies in the volumes *Birds, Beasts and Flowers*, which was published in 1923 and deals at times symbolically and at times descriptively with the natural world, and *Last Poems*, published posthumously in 1932, in which the writer movingly and honestly struggles to come to terms with the fact and imminence of death. The themes of the two volumes are, in fact, related, for to Lawrence death is seen as the natural balance of life, not something at which to be afraid. Without death, life could not go on, for as Lawrence himself sets out in the long essay 'Apropos of *Lady Chatterley's Lover*' the rhythm of the seasons is reflected in all life: whatever is decayed must be destroyed for the new vigorous life to be born. The sincerity of Lawrence's insistence throughout his life on the need for man to leave himself open to new experience and not to be afraid of the unknown is nowhere better confirmed than by the record of his own development set out in these later poems.

Birds, Beast and Flowers contains some of Lawrence's best poetry, particularly the poems 'Snake', 'Kangaroo', 'The Mosquito', 'Man and Bat' and 'Humming-Bird'. These poems succeed primarily because of the amazing ability which Lawrence had for realising what he himself referred to as 'the tremendous *non-human* quality of life', for establishing an understanding of the being of animals, and because through his reading of Whitman he had improved his own poetic techniques. In 'Snake', for example, it has been often pointed out that technically the use of the 's' alliteration combines wonderfully with the rhythmical movement of the lines to convey the slithering otherness of the snake:

> He reached down from a fissure in the earth-wall in the gloom
> And trailed his yellow-brown slackness so... ⁚ ...., over the
>   edge of the stone trough
> And rested his throat upon the stone bottom,
> And where the water had dripped from the tap, in a small clearness,
> He sipped with his straight mouth,
> Softly drank through his straight gums, into his slack long body,
>
> Silently.   p. 349

The poem as a whole, however, is such a brilliant success because, even if he never fully realised it elsewhere in his verse, Lawrence here not only handles the rhythms successfully but evokes dramatically the sense of atmosphere, the burning heat of a Sicilian summer, with the immediate realisation of an actual situation. The poet is here not preaching about the need for human awareness of the other animal world of nature, but presenting the reader with an actual situation in which the man's reaction is complicated: he sees the snake before him at the water-trough, and whilst one part of him admires and enters into an admiration of the otherness of the snake (the images relate it to 'a guest', 'a god', 'a king in exile') another part, 'the voice of my education', prompts him to kill it and arouses his innate fear. Many of these poems in the *Birds, Beasts and Flowers* volume involve this theme of the meeting of the human and non-human worlds of nature, but 'Snake' is so successful because of the honesty of the poet's response: the fear is genuine and understandable and yet, as the poem shows, petty. As the snake leaves, the man peevishly throws a log at it, and the action highlights the pettiness of that fear. 'Man and Bat' also deals with this theme of contact between man and creature, and the horror of realising the existence and proximity of the bat in the man's room is dramatically and vividly presented; but 'Snake' goes further, and qualifies our fear at some part of the world of nature in a remarkable way. However justified this fear may be at a superficial level, in another sense the fear is paltry and cheap, and 'Snake' conveys this sense of 'pettiness' with moving poetic insight.

In his *Last Poems* Lawrence is concerned at once with the themes of death and of rebirth. Many of these poems take on a poignancy in the light of the imminence of his own death which makes it difficult and perhaps almost distasteful to discuss them coldly in the light of their purely literary merit, although this is not to imply that they have none. 'Bavarian Gentians' has for long been highly praised, and some of those poems where Lawrence evokes a sense of the classical world of antiquity such as 'The Greeks are Coming', 'The Argonauts' and 'Middle of the World' are admirable in their power to suggest this past. Lawrence's new flowering of interest in this world of classical myth is characteristic of the man, and it is right that his last work should illustrate his openness to new experience of life and a willingness to accept the reality of death. The world of these *Last Poems* is a world of autumn and shadow mixed with an awareness of the significance of the myths of the past: of Persephone, symbolising the seasonal rebirth of nature, and of Venus Aphrodite, rising out of the sea. The recurrent images of the ship of death and

'The dark and endless ocean of the end'

are used by Lawrence not in any flamboyantly self-pitying or Tennysonian sense as in *In Memoriam* or *The Crossing of the Bar*. Self-pity and even egoism are markedly absent from these poems, and in them can be seen the theme which Lawrence had been re-iterating since *The Rainbow*: the need for man to submit to and accept the greater reality of nature. The dignity and sincerity of these last poems outweigh their occasional awkwardness of style and rhythm, for as James Reeves has well observed, in 'The Ship of Death' Lawrence 'turns his oldest and most persistent fault, that of repetitiveness, into a virtue, for here the repetition becomes a ritual incantation suggesting the solemnity of his own approaching end' (Introduction to Heinemann Poetry Bookshelf *Selected Poems of D. H. Lawrence*).

CONCLUSION

Lawrence's poetry on the whole suffers from a lack of control which is not typical of his major achievement as a novelist, but at the very least his poems do illustrate the integrity of his portrayal of experience. It is with such words as integrity and sincerity that Lawrence's work can be best summed up, for whatever blind spots there may have been in his attitude to life, the genuineness and freshness of his prose writing is a lasting testament to the degree of wholeness in him. Certainly in some of his work the despairing sense of urgency with which he stated the need to solve the problems of 20th-century industrial society strains the conception and execution of his major themes; but the flaws in his work arise from this urgency and concern, and not from an innate irrationality in his work or in himself. It should by now have been clearly shown in this study that Lawrence's concern was not solely with the primitive and uncivilised: rather he was passionately involved in an attempt to evolve a finer conception of reason by reconciling the violently separated worlds of nature and civilisation.

Nor is Lawrence unsophisticated or undisciplined as a writer. The notion of him as a raw untutored genius, current for so long, has little validity. His novels were written with painstaking care and are the result of considerable and inspired critical theorising by him on the novelist's art. His place in the history of the English novel is important, particularly in his development of techniques derived from the very different Russian and American traditions of the novel. His influence since his death on the novel has admittedly been slight. Angus Wilson has commented on

> the great stranded whale of D. H. Lawrence. Here is this vast and magnificent mammal that swam past us and yet the extraordinary thing is how few writers have been able to get much out of him.
>
> APPROACHES TO THE NOVEL, ed. J. Colmer, p. 30

Lawrence's reputation generally has been high of recent years, however, and this reputation has been based both on the importance of what he has to say for our civilisation and for the skill with which he says it. He may have failed to present an unanswerable argument against the artificial belief in reason and consciousness which typifies the worst aspects of modern civilisation, but his work can help to suggest ideas which could allow the reconstitution of reason upon a new basis and the achievement of a concept of humanity of greater profundity than we have known before.

Frieda Lawrence

Select Bibliography

This short list merely suggests some introductory reading and reference material. In addition, some of Lawrence's own essays are well worth reading. These can be found in *Phoenix* (edited by E. D. McDonald, Viking Press, New York, 1936), *Phoenix II* (edited by Warren Roberts and Harry T. Moore, Viking Press, 1968), *Selected Literary Criticism* (edited by Anthony Beal, Heinemann, 1955), and *Sex, Literature and Censorship* (Viking Press, New York).

LAWRENCE'S LIFE AND LETTERS

Edward Nehls: *D. H. Lawrence: A Composite Biography* (Univ. of Wisconsin Press, Madison, Wis., 1957-9). An excellent work of reference in three large volumes.

'E. T.' (Jessie Chambers): *D. H. Lawrence: A Personal Record* (Barnes & Noble, New York, 1965). A study of Lawrence's early career up to the *Sons and Lovers* period.

Harry T. Moore, ed.: *The Collected Letters of D. H. Lawrence* (2 vols. Viking Press, New York).

Richard Aldington's *D. H. Lawrence* (Macmillan, New York) and Harry T. Moore's *The Intelligent Heart* (Grove Press, New York, 1962) provide useful studies of Lawrence's life.

CRITICISM

F. R. Leavis: *D. H. Lawrence: Novelist* (Knopf, New York, 1956) remains by far the best critical work on Lawrence, and concentrates mainly on *The Rainbow*, *Women in Love*, and the stories.

Mary Freeman: *D. H. Lawrence: A Basic Study of his Ideas* (Grossett & Dunlap, New York).

David Gordon: *D. H. Lawrence as a Literary Critic* (Yale Univ. Press, New Haven, Conn. 1966).

H. M. Daleski: *The Forked Flame* (Northwestern Univ. Press, Evanston, Ill., 1965).

Keith Sagar: *The Art of D. H. Lawrence* (Cambridge Univ.Press, New York, 1966).

Mark Spilka: *The Love Ethic of D. H. Lawrence* (Indiana Univ. Press, Bloomington, Ind., 1955).

E. W. Tedlock, Jr.,: *D. H. Lawrence and 'Sons and Lovers': Sources and Criticisms* (New York Univ. Press, New York, 1965).

Included are excellent essays on the novel by Mark Schorer ('Technique as Discovery') and Dorothy Van Ghent.

Eliseo Vivas: *The Failure and the Triumph of Art* (Northwestern Univ. Press, Evanston, Ill., 1960).

Lawrence's poetry is well discussed in

W. H. Auden: *The Dyer's Hand* (Random House, New York, 1962).

Kenneth Young: *D. H. Lawrence* (London House, New York).

Index

Main entries are indicated by heavy type